THE GREEN VELVET DRESS

*Memories of
Sixty years
in London
and Somerset*

*The Author
in the Green Velvet Dress*

THE GREEN VELVET DRESS

*Memories of
Sixty years
in London
and Somerset*

KATHLEEN YOUNG

TALLIS PRESS

© Kathleen Young, 1989

Made and printed
in Great Britain
and published by
TALLIS PRESS
Whittingehame House
Haddington
East Lothian

ISBN 0284 98780 8

BY THE SAME AUTHOR
Beloved, Come Back

*For Bill & Reg
who are Tom & Nicholas*

Contents

	Wartime Introduction	ix
1	Childhood Days	1
2	School Days	16
3	Crays Hill	27
4	College and Early Teaching Days	35
5	Evacuation	44
6	Early Farming Days	56
7	Farming Tapestry	74
8	Changes in Farming	86
9	Leaving the Farm	94

Illustrations

The Author in the Green Velvet Dress	*Frontispiece*
My Mother	*Page* 4
My Grandma	4
Nicholas, my Brother, in his Seaford College uniform	6
My Father, killed in action at Poelcappelle, 1917	7
St Angela's Uniform — *we always wore gloves*	26
The Railway Carriage at Crays Hill	29
My Mother, my Brother and Myself at Walton-on-the-Naze	42
Tom and Myself on horseback	51
Lower Farm, Charterhouse	58
Charterhouse in the Winter of 1947	79
Scything Corn, which Tom can just remember	87
With a Class at Cheddar Primary School	94
Wanstead Cottage, Shipham	97

WARTIME INTRODUCTION

ONE EVENING during the Second World War, a few friends were sitting round a log fire in the drawing room of the vicarage in a remote village on the bleak Mendip Hills. The huge windows were noisy with the beating rain and the threshing of wind-tossed branches, shutting us in from the desolation of those lonely hills.

We had had supper on our knees, sardines on toast, a rare treat in those frugal years and were luxuriating in the warmth, talking about books, the stars, the latest rationing — about anything and everything. Suddenly, one of the party begged our hostess to "tell our fortunes — please, Millicent." (That is not her real name; in fact a most unlikely name, but it will do.)

Millicent was reluctant. She could tell fortunes with cards, but did not do so lightly; once begun, she knew she would become involved and unable to pass it off as a joke. However, she consented and someone fetched the cards. The party took it in a light-hearted way, chaffing each other till Millicent with a swift intake of breath, and a glance at her husband, rose abruptly and laid aside the cards. "Let's have some music," she said in a strained voice. "Come along," to one of her friends, "you play some choruses for us."

Years later, after her husband's early death, Millicent told me how she had seen death in his cards that night, sending a chill over her as he sat there joking.

I remember little of what Millicent told me except for one thing. She paused and said slowly, "you will get what you want — but you will have to wait a long time for it."

What *did* I want in those days? So many things! A wave of happiness engulfed me. So much time lay ahead filled with infinite possibilities. I could not choose just one thing.

How little I thought, when teaching in a quiet London suburb, how my life would change to that of living on an isolated Mendip farm with Italian and German prisoners of war sharing my home. Ernst, the German, once said, "I like to learn something new each day," a sentiment which I share. There is so much to learn, to read, to do, that the days are not long enough. Now I look forward with eager anticipation to reliving the good days with the bad. There have been grim, hard periods but each time we have emerged from the tunnel to happier times ahead.

CHAPTER ONE
Childhood Days

FAMILIAR SCENTS and sounds have the ability to transport one instantly to the world of childhood. The smell of frying steak; the scent of Old Man crushed between the fingers; the sound of wind whispering through poplar trees or the singing of "Where e'er you walk", are some of my magic carpets. And the enchanted numbers one, one, six are the invisible key to a suburban house on the outskirts of London.

In the bedroom of an as yet unfurnished house, stands a four-year-old girl with auburn curls beneath a pink sunbonnet, unaware that in a few months' time a baby brother would be born in that room.

For twenty five years, "116" was to be the focal point in the lives of those two children, Nicholas and myself. At the edge of the London area it was fringed by the outlying parts of Epping Forest. At one end of our avenue lay Wanstead Park, haunt of childhood with a never-ending series of delights. Armed with a jam-jar hanging from a string tied round the neck and a bamboo cane with a fishing net on the end, we fished for tiddlers which were singularly hard to catch, but with the expectancy of childhood we kept on trying.

There were picnics in the shady woods and ball games on the grassy places between lake and woods. Once, greatly daring, for we were not supposed to venture so far alone, we set off to walk right round the Ornamental Water. We walked hand-in-hand, past the long disused boathouse and the grotto built beside the water, near the pillared ruins of the former Wanstead House. Ducks and moorhens glided silently through the dark waters which reflected the surrounding trees. Overhead, herons flew with feet outstretched behind, to their nests on the thickly wooded island. It was very quiet. The path seemed endless as the edge of the lake curved to form little bays and inlets. We tightened our grip. Still only halfway round. Supposing the path did not go all the way? The way back seemed endless too, so we plodded on with fast-beating hearts. There was a bridge! We ran the last few yards and our footsteps echoed hollowly on the wooden planks spanning a narrow neck of the lake. A quick run through the more familiar woodland took us to the sunny glade where families picnicked and children shouted in their play. Whether I was punished for taking Nicholas so far into the forbidden woods I do not know, but there was no need. I would not venture again into that dark, silent world beyond the Ornamental Water!

In the well-trodden woods around the keepers' cottages we were never afraid. We knew every little winding path between the rhododendron bushes with their pale mauve flowers and the leafy caves beneath the bushes ideal for playing hide-and-seek. Here grew the pale bluebells so different from the deep-purple bells later found on Mendip.

In autumn came the big red hawthorn berries to be threaded with darning wool and needle to make necklaces, and fat acorns which, when balanced on the neck of a water-filled medicine bottle, produced the miracle of roots and shoots later transplanted to the end of the garden to make a miniature oak forest behind the white-heart cherry tree.

But best of all were the smooth, shiny horse-chestnuts whose beauty brought the greatest joy, tantalising and transient. I was consumed with a desire to do something with the lovely things, to identify myself with them in some mysterious way. Those magical horse-chestnuts remain the symbol of the desire to experience nature, to get into the sea rather than sit and look at it, to handle stones and find fossils, to explore winding tracks across rough gorse and heather-clad hill sides. Trees, hedges, rough stone walls, the wind and the rain, primroses and deep snow, are an endless source of delight filled with the same yearning for something beyond "the long littleness of life".

At the other end of the avenue lay Wanstead Flats. The lake here was more ordinary than those in the park, surrounded by sand-hills, lovely for running up and down. We called it "Swan Lake" for, one year, the stately pair of swans gathered rushes with their beaks to make a huge mound for a nest. We watched daily while the pen sat until a train of browny-grey cygnets appeared, swimming in line behind their parents.

To walk across the Flats to the station, or to catch a bus at Manor Park not only saved a halfpenny return ticket, but was delightful when the hawthorn bushes were in sweetly-scented blossom. The end of our avenue was the terminus of the tram line. Here, the driver jumped out with a long pole in his hand, with which he hooked the arm from the overhead wire, transferring it to the wire at the other end of the vehicle. Then he mounted the other end of the tram and set off with a rattle and clang towards Woolwich Docks. Inside, the passengers sat facing each other on the long, shiny, slatted wooden seats, but upstairs the seats were arranged in pairs and the backs could be swivelled across according to the direction of travel. On opentopped trams macintosh covers could be pulled over the knees.

Opposite the lake were the shops which we knew as "up top". Between the baker's and the butcher's stood Hardings, a long, narrow draper's and haberdasher's. Near the entrance one bought reels of black and white cotton, linen buttons which did not break when mangled, black and white tape, elastic, safety pins and hair-pins. Then came the section devoted to ladies' underwear, where combinations, chemises and Liberty bodices were kept in long fitments. I do not remember buying petticoats: they were made at home by Grandma.

Long before the appearance of departmental stores in our area this emporium was personally supervised by Miss Harding and her sister Miss Edith. Each wore a high-necked white blouse tucked into an ankle-length black skirt, each with grey hair piled into a "chelsea bun" on the top of the head. It was a great adventure to accompany Grandma on a shopping expedition to buy calico for her chemises — which she would not dream of buying ready-made — while I might choose the narrow embroidered edging. Here, too, Grandma bought the narrow-striped calico, blue or pink and white, for our sailor blouses. Nicholas was lucky. He always had a real whistle hanging on a cord round his neck and tucked into his pocket.

At our entrance, Miss Edith came from behind the counter to place chairs at strategic points, for shopping was a leisurely

Grandma   *My Mother*

business. Our great joy was to watch how the money and the bill were placed in a little, round, wooden box which was then screwed on to a lid which hung on a wire overhead. When Miss Harding pulled a wooden handle the container whizzed along the overhead wires to a glass cubby-hole where Mr Harding, father of the two ladies, sat. With a pull of his handle the box with receipted bill and change sped back to stop above Miss Harding's head. With material at a shilling three-farthings a yard and ribbon at three-farthings a yard there was often a farthing in the change. When this little coin was in short supply, a paper of pins, a pastel-coloured strip with a neat row of pins, was offered instead.

One winter while I was at High School, Grandma emerged with a large brown paper parcel which Grandpa carried home for her. On Christmas morning each of my aunts, my mother and myself were presented with parcels of identical size. This was an amazing departure from the usual handing round of a half-crown (12½p) each and the presents were given to us when the men of the family were in the front room. We carefully

4

untied the string and opened the brown paper to find two pairs of navy blue Chilpruf bloomers.

"I find them very comfortable," explained Grandma. "You will be well set up now and they will last you for years." They did. Mine saw me through school and even accompanied me to college to wear under a gymslip for P.E. One did not buy new garments in those days until the old were past repair.

These superior bloomers had little rosettes of navy ribbon on each leg at the join of the elastic, which marked them out from plebian garments at half the price. This rosette proved invaluable to my mother when one of her pairs disappeared. My mother was not a tidy person, but try as she would they could not be found. In those days we had a domestic help known in the family as "the little lady". Small, wispy-haired, incompetent, she was employed mainly as an excuse for my mother to give her money, for the house never looked any different when she had finished. One day, however, she was sweeping under a bed — or at least raising a dust — when mother noticed and recognised the rosettes on the kneeling knickered legs.

"Those are my bloomers!" she exclaimed indignantly and made the woman change into a less aristocratic pair.

At about that time there was a beige costume on show at Harding's, priced at thirty shillings. After much deliberation it was decided that I should spend my Christmas presents from my two Uncles — a pound note and a ten shilling note — on it. But alas! The notes had disappeared from the desk on the top of the chest of drawers where I had kept them. My mother guessed where the money had gone; the "little lady" was sent packing and I was given the money to buy the coat and skirt.

Hitherto, Grandma had made my coats, often from carefully unpicked garments discarded by my aunts. This was my first grown-up costume. Brilliant flesh-coloured silk stockings (salmon pink as I remember them), with pointed black patent shoes, replaced the black woollen school stockings and tie-up shoes every Sunday. With a wide-brimmed, light brown straw hat trimmed with narrow red and green velvet, I had reached the height of elegance. I wore, of course, fine kid gloves. These had to be blown into on removal to retain their shape when laid

*Nicholas, my Brother, in his
Seaford College uniform*

away till the following Sunday. During the week they were replaced by white cotton gloves.

My father remains a shadowy figure of whom a few memories stand out with the clarity of brilliantly coloured miniatures. I see him at Saturday dinner time with little silver-wrapped packets of Five Boys chocolate tied with narrow ribbon, or sometimes, as a special treat, a bar of Fry's chocolate cream each.

But he was whisked away to the army by, I was sure, the alarming man who pointed from the posters and declared, "Your Country Needs YOU!" My mother and I watched

My Father,
killed in action at Poelcappelle, 1917

from the dining-room window as Dad walked away in his Royal Field Artillery uniform.

"Why don't you cry?" I asked. Only later did I discover that our family never cried before each other. Superhuman efforts were made to refrain from tears until one was alone.

Once Dad appeared overnight in the big double bed beside

my little one. On my pillow lay "Betty", a flat, printed rag doll with her name on her back. Sellotape covers the split in her printed check rompers now, to prevent the sawdust running out, and the marks are still on her head where I tried to pin my own auburn curls, ruthlessly "bobbed" by my Aunt Vi. In Nicholas' cot lay "Sailor Boy".

Then the final memory concerning my father. Grandma and I were standing inside the privet hedge surrounding our front garden when a neighbour passed.

"You know Fred's gone?" said Grandma.

I was too young to understand the import of her words. Dad, a gunner in the Royal Field Artillery, had been killed in action and has no known grave. Just ten days before the outbreak of the Second World War, my mother was taken to see his name on a memorial near Poperinghe.

Shortly after that day in the garden I was standing in the infants' school cloakroom while a sympathetic teacher knelt to button my navy serge coat. Grandma had made it and I liked the little grey squirrel collar made from a scrap of fur, but she had economically covered button moulds with the rough serge which set my teeth on edge when they were forced through the button holes. We were going for a holiday in the country with Auntie Vi.

"Is your mother taking you for good?" enquired the teacher.

"Of course!" I replied indignantly. As though my mother would do anything "for bad" I thought!

Now that our mother was a war widow decisions had to be taken; Grandpa paid off the outstanding £100 on our house which was a large sum in those days, and my mother obtained a job in the Japanese Bank in which my father had worked. As a girl she had entered for the Civil Service examination and she often told me how, on the day of the interview, she had a bad cough. Determined not to miss the chance she also determined not to cough and was accepted. Her work in the Post Office involved relief duty at Barbican and Mount Pleasant Central Post offices and Uncle Jim, her brother, used to tell us how he had glimpsed his sister coping efficiently with mounds of parcels — rather to his surprise. At Clark's College our mother learnt the regular style of handwriting and impeccable spelling which remained with her until her death at eighty-three.

We children went to Grandma's for the day: Nicholas was two years old and I was attending the elementary infants' school. At Grandma's we were well trained; toys put tidily away; crumbs dropped at meal-times swept up with brush and dustpan. At dinner we were expected to eat some of every dish offered and large tapioca was my main difficulty, it was so hard to swallow. But at teatime this had advantages; after the bread and butter stage, all biscuits and cakes might be sampled.

Grandpa, in black suit and bowler hat, departed each morning to the Goldsmith's Hall. In those days, before radio, Grandma was time-keeper. She checked the gold watch, hanging on a chain round her neck and tucked into a little pocket, with Grandpa who had checked with the station clock. Every morning she called up the stairs, "It wants three minutes to the half hour, Jim!" Grandpa was never late for the 8.49 train to Liverpool Street. He was interested in his grandchildren and tried to share his skill in pen and ink drawing with us. He also tried to teach me Rule of Three from an ancient arithmetic book — without much success!

Grandma could still quote the answers to questions in *A Child's Guide to Knowledge*. The book was inscribed, "Miss Dear, October 1871" when Grandma was nine years old. A pencil mark, a tick and date until the completion in 1874. "What is cochineal?" I asked when helping to ice a cake. "A very beautiful scarlet dye," came the prompt reply, "produced from insects about the size of a pea, which are only found in Mexico and New Spain." Then the book was brought out. A mine of information learnt by little girls by question and answer over a hundred years ago. I have the book still.

Life was a dreadful rush for my mother. In contrast to her efficiency at work, in the house she had "no method" as my practical Grand-mother used to say. Coming home from a day's work she must collect us children, light the fire — no central heating in those days — prepare the tea, do the housework, wash the clothes, all without the help of gadgets taken for granted today. Vacuum cleaners had not been heard of: those were the days of brush and dustpan and of beating carpets upon the clothes' line with a cane beater.

There were no detergents. Washing was done in the galvanised bath with a handful of soda and a bar of Sunlight or Lifebuoy soap. Washing machines had not been invented. When "whites" were to be boiled, the fire was lit beneath the copper built into the corner of the scullery, to heat the water drawn from the tap over the sink. The mangle with its wooden rollers, screwed down when in use, was kept outside — it was too big for the scullery.

When it came to the ironing, the flat-irons were hung on an iron bracket in front of the barred grate in the kitchen and reheated when they cooled. The miracle of an electric iron lay in the distant future.

When the roaring monster of a geyser was installed in the bathroom I was terrified of it, fearing that the thing would explode. But it did save dependence on the erratic boiler behind the kitchen fire, or the carrying of hot water to the bedroom where the green china jugs with pink roses stood in their basins on the washstand.

Each morning the doorstep must be whitened with "whitening" and every self-respecting housewife should, according to Grandma, clean her brass doorknocker and letter-box before breakfast. (But brass stair-rods needed to be removed and polished only once a week. Thursday was Grandma's stair-rod day.)

Finally there was me to be got ready and sent off to school and Nicholas to be delivered to Grandma's in his push-chair before the run across the Flats to the station for the 8.41 train. A day's work in the routine of the telephonists' office in the Bank must have seemed like a rest.

Despite the rush of everyday life, our mother still found time for worship and Sundays followed a regular pattern. We all went to Matins and Evensong; it was taken for granted that we went but we found it no great burden. There was always a hot roast dinner and in the afternoons Sunday school and then Bible Class — until our late teens when our time became our own. Then our mother continued her Sunday school class, a slender figure in dark green chenille velvet dress with flying side panels, broad brimmed, black straw hat and pointed black shoes on the feet which later became so crippled. Mother had few new clothes; most of the money went on us children, but when occasion arose she bought something "good" which lasted for years and gave her an air of elegance.

The Sunday school children loved her, avidly collecting the texts which I was deputed to buy in sheets and cut up each week. She caused herself endless trouble in trying to persuade the superintendent to give party tickets to boys who, he said, attended only when party time drew near, feeling sure, as she put it, that it would encourage them to continue to attend. Sometimes it did. One of those boys, then a man, wrote to us on her death, "She was the champion of the outcast, the unacceptable", he said, "I shall never forget her".

Unconventional as she was, people in trouble always came to our mother, taking hours of her time in pouring out their woes and going away comforted with a half-crown in their pockets.

The way our mother carried her faith into her daily life while rarely speaking of religion; this interweaving of the spiritual and material, was perhaps the greatest of her gifts to her children.

Suddenly this life of peaceful Sundays and frantic weekdays changed. Mother gave up her job in the Bank — something to do with obtaining a place for Nicholas at a public school.

It must have been a terrible wrench to see her son, aged ten, who had never left home alone, thrust into the world of school so far away. There was, of course, no car in which to run down to Sussex at weekends and the train journey was too expensive for more than one visit a term. At the same time she lost the companionship of her colleagues and the stimulus of the work she loved, as well as half her income.

There was another problem which haunted her lonely way. For years she was inexplicably torn between her love for the Church of England, never missing a service, and the urgent inner call to join the Roman Catholic church. She went to Lourdes and to Rome for the Holy Year, always alone. She was instructed in the Catholic faith and when I entered the Ursuline Convent on a scholarship at Forest Gate she even had me instructed. Then she suddenly withdrew me, feeling it was not right to solve her problem through me. But I am glad to have had that early introduction since many of my friends in later life have been Catholics.

The stumbling block to her being "received" on each occasion was that she could not in conscience declare our church to be totally wrong. At last mother met a priest who did not require this declaration and she slipped quietly into the Catholic church. Now Grandma must be told. It must have been intensely difficult to face that matriarchal figure and incur her displeasure. "Oh, I wouldn't," was Grandma's reaction to anything beyond her accepted code, exerting tremendous influence on her family, the possessive mother who never let her children be free to live their own lives. But the deed was done. Nicholas and I in late teens felt embarrassed and continued in our original loyalty. My mother was never a conventional Catholic: she was before her time and in the simplest way was above rules and regulations.

Our mother was very easy to hurt, very easily squashed by conventionally minded people, nevertheless she had an inner strength. She always tried to help the less fortunate. There was a little girl of illiterate parents who could not learn at school and who came every day to "help Mum" as she put it. Somehow in this loving atmosphere, spelling as they worked or walked to the shops, she began to read. Later she married the milkman and raised a happy family.

Mother's secret was the giving of time to those in need, a more costly gift than money, with the result that she rarely had time to do the things she loved, to read or to go to an occasional play at the Old Vic. She was generous to a fault, maddeningly so to us more ordinary folk. When the Church sent her a Harvest basket later in life, she immediately gave the apples to children, the sugar to Mrs B. and there was always something that Grandma would like. In our younger days Nicholas and I had to help to decorate and fill strawberry baskets with fruit and vegetables for children whose mothers did not bother, so that they too, might have an offering to take to the Harvest Festival.

There were animals too. Our Gingers and Blackies were all strays who developed into much loved, well fed cats. She would spend one and sixpence ($7\frac{1}{2}$p), a large sum on a small income, on fish for the cats and the fishman gave her huge fish heads to boil. How I hated the job of removing the bones when occasionally moved to help! She was fearless in speaking up for an ill-treated horse or dog, to the acute embarrassment of her children. Some milkmen were cross when the horse stopped at our gate and looked enquiringly round for his lump of sugar.

Number "116" was a solid type of suburban semi-detached house. The dining-room on the right of the long hall was rarely used except for visitors, but the table in the bay window was crowded with pots of fern, little cacti and two large aspidistras.

"Coo! A bloomin' green 'ouse!" commented one urchin, with his jar of tiddlers plodding home from the park. Mother's pride and joy was a velota lily which still blooms regularly in August. At the end of the long corridor was the drawing-room, rather dark as it led into the conservatory. Here, too, was a miscellaneous collection of plants, and vases of chinese lanterns, lavender and fading flowers all gathering dust but never thrown away. One tended to put things in the drawing room "for the time being", out of the way and then forget them.

But the heart of the house was the kitchen, not very well-named, for the cooking and washing-up were done in the scullery. It was a comfortable room with an open grate, large wooden table and dresser. The table was usually crowded with things not put away as they would be needed shortly. There was not much room in the cupboards and drawers anyway, for my mother never discarded anything which might prove remotely useful. Little jars, lids, chipped crocks, saucers in which to stand plants, were all preserved until the magic moment for their use arrived: and then the object in question could not be found.

But there were times, mostly Saturday afternoons, which stand out as oases of peace and quietness in the kitchen. When the table had been miraculously cleared and spread with the red and green patterned chenille table-cloth, the fire glowed in the red tiled grate, my mother for once relaxed and engrossed in a book and I sat at the table lost in a world of ice and snow. Here I followed the steps of Scott and Amundsen, lived through the Polar night "Alone" with Sir Douglas Mawson and climbed impossible peaks in the Himalayas with F. S. Smythe, while the clock ticked loudly and cinders dropped through the grate.

Here it was too, that the Christmas puddings were made. Dried fruit must be washed, raisins stoned, suet from the butcher shredded and the candied peel yielded its delicious centre of sugar to be shared among the children. Then, everything was chopped with the wooden-handled blade or minced in the heavy iron mincer screwed to the table, before the mixing and final stirring with a secret wish, in the large green wash-basins with pink roses from the bedroom; the largest bowls available. The puddings were boiled all day in the copper and preparations begun for making mincemeat. Neither my mother nor Grandma ever *bought* pudding or mincemeat.

Treats in those days were few and simple, looked forward to for weeks ahead. In November we watched the post for Uncle Harold's letter inviting us to the pantomime with our two cousins, followed by weeks of anticipation. My first pantomime was Cinderella, with its miracle of the transformation scene and the ballet which followed. The pantomime was always at the Lyceum followed by an Underground train journey to spend the night with our cousins, where we re-enacted the scenes; the boys being slap-stick clowns and the girls ballet dancers. Round the piano we sang the comic song of the day! "Yes, we have no bananas" was one of my favourites. So ended a perfect day. A whole year seemed a very long time to wait for our next pantomime.

A smaller treat occurred twice each November on the birthdays of Grandma and Uncle Jim. At teatime we waited expectantly for Auntie Ger to come home from the City with two cardboard boxes containing cream buns. Enormous, they seemed; filled with delicious fresh cream to be eaten and savoured at every slow mouthful. I do not think we had a cream bun during the other months. Christmas was magical, beginning during the previous week with the Salvation Army Band playing Advent carols in the road at night, raising expectation to fever pitch.

On Christmas morning it was a point of honour not to open our stockings and parcels before our mother reached home from the 6 o'clock service — but just feeling in the dark was delightful. In the toe was always a sugar mouse with a string tail, a new penny wrapped in silver paper and an orange. Oranges were in the shops only around Christmastime in those days, a real treat.

After church at 11 a.m., we carried our presents round to Grandma's in half a cane dress basket each, for a day of fun and games, each singing a song or reciting a poem. Surprisingly, it was we children who bought the Christmas tree from our hoarded pocket money and a present for each adult from Woolworth's, the "Nothing over sixpence" ($2\frac{1}{2}$p) store. After tea, with the lights out we lit the little coloured candles, shining on the tinsel and coloured glass balls, and distributed our gifts to Grandma and Grandpa, our mother and our aunts and uncles.

CHAPTER TWO

School Days

MY EARLIEST MEMORIES of infant school centre round an enormous shiny rocking horse in the hall. It was painted white with black patches and had a bristling black mane and long flowing tail. We longed to have a ride as a reward for good work or behaviour, but when the moment came for teachers to lift the child on to its back, with feet firmly fixed in the stirrups, it was terrifying to be perched so high above the other children. When at last my turn came I clung desperately to the reins, fearful of slipping off its back or of gliding over its head to the floor. Nonetheless, it was a moment of triumph to be savoured after, rather than during, the event.

On Friday afternoons we were each issued with a wooden box containing two-inch cane beads and many coloured, round glass ones. A needle threaded with strong twine with a bead tied to the end was supplied. The idea was to thread long and short beads alternately on to the twine to be hung to make curtains which rattled as one passed through. Try as one might, it was impossible to fill two threads in the time allotted and at the sound of the bell rung in the hall, we must unthread the unfinished string. As no new curtains ever appeared in the school, I guess the teacher rapidly slid the beads off each string after school, re-threading the needles for next week's "lesson".

As for learning to read, I have no clear memory. At school, since I was already able to read, the brown, soft-covered books, each page with a picture at the top to illustrate such mysteries as, "Can the ox get a box?" presented no difficulties. I did not connect this activity with reading — that was done at home with my own books — but was something mysteriously connected with going to school. Much later, I have a frustrating memory of being issued with a copy of *The Old*

Curiosity Shop on Friday afternoon. Most of the pages were loose and hopelessly out of order, and I spent much of the precious half-hour frantically trying to make order out of chaos and read a little more of the story before the inevitable bell rang. There was no school library, of course. A visit to the public library involved a long walk down Rabbits Road, past the cemetery to Manor Park — but there was no book to be seen. Instead, catalogues were laid on counters, rather like pattern books today, and one searched for a likely-looking title and then went to the walls, where the numbers were displayed on movable slots operated from the office. If the number was red, the book was available and one went to the librarian's window to ask for it; if black, the book was already on loan and the process started again. But at home we were fortunate; our father had collected rows of leather bound classics, Trollope, Dickens, Mrs Henry Wood, Wilkie Collins, and Grandpa lent me Scott's novels. I particularly enjoyed *The Talisman*. I cried over *A Peep Behind the Scenes* and *Christy's Old Organ*, relics from my mother's childhood with *Beau Brocade* and *The Scarlet Pimpernel*. On one auspicious birthday Auntie Vi gave me *What Katy Did* combined with *What Katy Did Next*, a truly superior volume! Then there was *Little Women*. How I admired Jo and longed to be like her, for she had long curly, red hair and, best of all, wrote stories!

One holiday, soon after starting school, Mother, Nicholas and I spent a holiday at Bognor with our cousins. One early morning before breakfast my cousin and I were taken to bathe in the sea. This sticks in my memory only because on our return home we were both struck with some mysterious illness — probably nothing to do with bathing! I remember a specialist telling mother, "Of course, she can walk!" As a result, I joined four or five other little girls who shared a governess. Each morning we met her at our homes in turn, carrying a book of our own choice. Miss Miller was a good teacher. We hurried through our sums and spellings, to get to the point at which we could remove our book markers and struggle willingly with long words in order to enjoy the story.

So the work when I joined the junior school held no terrors. The classrooms were around the central hall in the building beneath the junior boys, and we had separate playgrounds. There was a long shed in the playground with a wall seat, into which we crowded during wet playtimes. No one thought of keeping us indoors when it rained.

Morning and afternoon the school bell, pulled by a big girl in the top class, sounded over the neighbourhood. During the "firstie" we ambled along, chatting as friends joined the group, but should the "secondy" start before we reached the playground, there was a rush to reach our lines before a teacher emerged to inspect the silent columns. At the clap of her hands we marched decorously into school.

Games came and went according to the season, changing abruptly without apparent volition. At one time it would be wooden tops which boys and girls alike wound with a piece of string and set spinning. Then, for girls, skipping ropes were "in". A length of old clothes-line was carried to school, or, the height of luxury, a yellow-handled rope with the possible refinement of ball bearings in each handle. With a long rope we played "Follow my Leader". "Salt, Mustard, Vinegar, Pepper" was a great favourite, the rope turned very fast for pepper, and "Over the Water" meant running in against the direction of the turning rope, one jump and out again. Bumps were the fashion too. The rope was turned very fast so that one jumped over a couple of turns. This could be played in a group with two turners or with one's own rope.

Suddenly ropes were left at home and hopscotch was the rage. Our suburban pavements lent themselves to the step-jump with widespread feet. But first a stone must be thrown into each square in sequence so that one turned where it lay. We were lucky to have such pavements, for drawing squares with chalk would never have been allowed.

Hoops were fun, though they could not be taken to school. Boys had iron hoops with an iron skillet hooked at the end, but, for the girls, there were wooden hoops of varying sizes bowled along with a wooden hoop stick with a small knob at the end.

Balls for bouncing, old tennis balls or hollow rubber ones apt to burst, were another craze; bouncing to see who could keep it up the longest or throwing games in pairs, keeping two balls in the air. There was great excitement when the first Sorbo balls appeared in the shops. Coloured red, blue, green or yellow they were made of spongy material and bounced high over one's head; but they cost a shilling, so my weekly twopence were saved for six weeks before I could carry off my green treasure from the newsagent's shop. It gave endless pleasure. We had tennis rackets and the boys had cricket bats, and our brothers played marbles and five stones while we skipped and bounced. We had a scooter, too and with one foot on the scooter propelled ourselves forward by the other foot; but we were warned to use feet alternately, not to wear out one shoe before the other. My cousins had the refinement of a scooter propelled with an up-and-down pedal, but we never aspired to such heights, though they did let us have a turn during visits. Then there were group games; Tag, Statues and Giants' Strides, when the girl in front turned suddenly and caught anyone moving, were favourite games and also Twos and Threes. There were always groups of girls playing games if no other craze was in.

My friends and I were avid readers of Angela Brazil's school stories about boarding schools, passing a book carefully from friend to friend. Then we acted them, each taking a character and embroidering the story on our way home from school or on Saturday mornings on Wanstead Flats. Occasionally we had a "feast", each girl contributing some delicacy; a twist of coconut or a few sultanas wheedled from mother when baking. Marjorie from the baker's shop, a pale girl with tight yellow ringlets, sometimes brought stale cakes or buns, all eaten with relish and a sip of sherbet water.

During the long winter evenings before the advent of wireless or television, we read or played Snakes and Ladders, Ludo, draughts, Halma and Dominoes, and there was always our piano practice.

It was round about 1930 that we had our first wireless set, made by a neighbour. Nicholas saw it first and intrigued me with his description of "a big piece of cheese!" It *was* wedge-shaped: a varnished wooden box on the sloping front of which were a couple of knobs and the cat's whisker — a little bit of wire which was directed on to the crystal and moved around to get the best reception. Attached to the side by a long cord was a pair of headphones. These were used in turn or could be unscrewed so that two people could listen at once. Sometimes one would be listening when the front door bell rang. Jumping up impulsively one found the whole set swinging in mid-air, suspended between the wall and the earphones on one's head. The call sign 2LO heralded mostly musical programmes at first, but Children's Hour was popular, headed by Uncle Mac, famous as Larry the Lamb, and Commander Stephen King-Hall, who gave talks on current affairs.

Years later, Grandma had one of the first commercial wireless sets — which still had a lot of wires about it — and still used earphones. But this set had two pairs and on the occasion of King George V's and Queen Mary's Silver Jubilee, Grandma and I returned from church and then spent the whole day with earphones on so as not to miss a moment of this hitherto unheard-of occasion.

Later, loudspeakers were introduced and Grandma had a set, but she considered the loudspeaker too noisy so we continued to sit solemnly around the table with earphones. By the time Grandma was ninety, television had arrived and her neighbours were fore-runners in the road in possessing a set. Grandma was persuaded to go in and view the Coronation of Queen Elizabeth but I think she would rather have been listening on earphones.

Silent films were shown in cinemas in my young days but I was not allowed to go very often for fear of picking up germs in the crowded atmosphere, so that the few occasions when friends or relatives took us to see Charlie Chaplin stand out as highlights. A woman sat at the piano with eyes fixed on the scene, suiting the music to sad or gay scenes, with a crescendo of chords and runs to accompany scenes of action, low sweet music for the love scenes. One had to be a good reader to follow the conversation dubbed below the picture. It was maddening to hear people sitting behind, reading stumblingly to their neighbours. During the interval the brightly-lit organ rose mysteriously to fill the whole building with music, in turn plaintive and tremulant or deep-voiced and throbbing, as the organist ran through the gamut of stops before disappearing into the depths with a final burst of sound.

May Day at the junior school was a day to be prepared for weeks beforehand. Each class learnt a country dance and we were solemnly asked whether our party frocks — always white or cream — had a blue or a pink sash, for no party dress was complete without one, and we danced boy or girl accordingly. My sash was always pink.

One year, Grandma made my sailor blouses in stiff narrow-striped denim with knickers to match; rather long-legged with a band round the lower edges. I went through hours of misery in those knickers. No matter how I tried to turn them up so that they squeezed my thighs, they always came down as I danced and showed as my skirt swayed with the motion. How I longed for my white knickers with elastic in the legs for every-day wear — but they were reserved for best and I do not think it ever occurred to me to ask to wear them to school.

One ticket was given to each child for the afternoon or evening ceremony. For some reason, I was surreptitiously slipped two, one for Grandma and one for my mother, for the afternoon and evening performances. Each girl took a bunch of flowers and groceries for the hospital, to be laid at the feet of the May Queen to the tune of "Where e're you walk!" To be May Queen was the highest honour the school could offer, she was watched in her traditional robes with awe-struck admiration by the younger fry.

The maypole was intricately woven into a tent of ribbons by the top class while Miss Fryer energetically played the piano. Our opening song "All is bright and cheerful round us," was sung to the tune of "Alleluia! alleluia! Hearts to heaven and voices raise," which has since been my favourite Easter hymn. The opening bars played by the organist transport me immediately to the hall of Aldersbrook Junior Girls' School.

Next door to Grandma lived Marie, youngest of a long family, and we played endless games of Mothers and Fathers in her garden, the chief attraction of which was a dug-out made by her father for protection during the First World War. Whether it was ever used for its original purpose I do not know, but it made a splendid cold storage for butter, milk and meat and provided us with a creepy hideaway for secret talks.

One day, Marie had to come and play in Grandma's garden, for her sister was to have her tonsils and adenoids removed by the local doctor as she lay on the sitting-room table. Marie managed to slip home, ostensibly to get a doll but really to peep through the window, and came back with a lurid story of the floor "swimming in blood".

One fateful day I was playing with Jennie, who lived next door to 116, and had been expressly forbidden to take my new china doll out of doors. Succumbing to Jennie's pleas I fetched her. The doll was dropped and her head smashed to pieces. Though the Dolls' Hospital supplied a new head she was never the same. Disobedience brought its own reward.

We had a hammock slung between the pear and cherry trees where, with a book, I swung long summer afternoons away. Nicholas and I sometimes made a tent with a sheet slung across a rope tied between the apple tree and a chair, and anchored with stones. It was fun furnishing our home with things brought from indoors, but not so good when they must all be taken in and put away.

At nine years old I jumped a standard and so was among girls older than myself. The work presented no difficulties but there were other snags. Three afternoons a week we had an hour's needlework. In the lower classes this had been enjoyable, choosing coloured silks and making mats and brush and comb bags with rows of parallel stitches with cross-stitches in between. But in Standard Four we learnt strictly practical sewing; tacking, running, hemming, leading to French seam and run-and-fell seams. Then we progressed to patches showing a square on the right side set with rows of nearly invisible stitches, and darning for which we brought a piece of woollen vest. A good darn had a close lattice of wool with even loops on each edge. Finally came setting into a band. A six-inch square of calico must be run, drawn up, stroked and each tiny resulting fold hemmed into a folded band.

This was the examination exercise set one winter's day as I sat at the back left-hand corner of the stepped classroom, and it provided the severest temptation of my young life. Try as I would, my specimen became a grubby, crumpled, blood-stained rag, wetted by surreptitious tears. To give more time there was no play, but girls were sent out in turn to be excused. The girl beside me went out and there on her desk was a perfect piece of work, spotlessly clean. Should I change it for mine? Fortunately common sense prevailed. One can imagine the uproar which would have resulted, but for the moment it was a very real temptation!

At last we graduated, at ten years old, to making raglan calico nightdresses for ourselves. We did not cut them out, of course; girls were assessed as small, medium or big and issued with a garment. First there were the endless run-and-fell seams, each to be tacked, run, turned, tacked and hemmed and then the bottom to hem. The neck and sleeves were to be scalloped. Being younger, I was not considered capable of drawing my own scallops round a halfpenny and, to my dismay, the older girl did not make the corners of the neckline scallops match. In fear and trembling I approached Mrs A whose forbidding appearance, grey hair drawn severely into a bun, steel-rimmed spectacles and rasping voice, struck terror into my heart. Miraculously, she smiled and with rubber and pencil soon put the matter right: that smile was like the warmth of a summer day after a sharp frost.

Another day, we had a painting examination. The model was a vase of sweet peas and I industriously set to work. Alas! Nothing went right! In panic I spread layer over layer of watercolour till there was nothing but muddy brown daubs. Two days later when each painting was held up for comment, beginning with the best, and marks were awarded, I went through half an hour of pure hell. Now was the moment when mine must be exhibited. I stared at my desk, digging my nails into my palms, determined not to cry, when the dreaded voice said kindly, "Well that's all." How kind Mrs A. was! I loved her from that moment.

At the age of eleven came the scholarship. Only promising children, or those whose parents insisted upon their entering, sat this. Most of my class lived in Wanstead and so had to sit at the High School there. Our house was just in the borough of East Ham, so I had to set off alone with ruler, rubber, pencil and a pen with a new nib in my violet leather pencil case, to the ordeal, knowing no-one in the barrack-like technical school.

Despite a severe attack of nerves a letter later informed my mother that I had obtained a scholarship for the Tech or for St Angela's Ursuline Convent High School, Forest Gate. Joyfully, my mother accepted the latter, being drawn to the Catholic faith and, I suspect, secretly hoping that somehow this would be a step nearer.

In September I accordingly set out in tussore blouse, brown serge pinafore dress, cotton gloves and, crowning glory, a brown mortar board! How proud I was of that mortar board! It must never be worn at a rakish angle, and pupils were expected to behave in the street in a manner conforming to one's uniform. One *never* ate an ice-cream in the street.

Most girls had long hair and two plaits, not one, were de rigueur, tied with size 9 or 16 black hair ribbon. Mine was not long enough to plait, indeed scarcely long enough to be tied into two bunches since I had been "bobbed" by my aunt. I adored long curly hair. Stella, in my class, had the most beautiful, deep auburn natural curls. Nevertheless, Stella too must have plaits, so her mother cut it, for everyone knew that to plait curly hair made it straight. How I grieved with Stella for the loss of those lovely curls and agreed passionately when she said, "If God had meant me to have straight hair, He would have given it to me," but rules were rules in those days.

At junior school we had learnt only script but at St Angela's we were expected to do cursive writing. The class prefect from the sixth form set us a copy each for homework and we learnt to write by laboriously copying such maxims as "A stitch in time saves nine" or "Satan finds work for idle hands." Fountain pens were not allowed; we still used steel nibs and bottles of ink in the first form.

For gym we changed into the more usual pleated gymslips, brown not the common navy serge, a decorous two inches above the knee. Once, I forgot mine and Uncle Jim walked all the way across the Flats to bring it for me, thus saving me from detention for carelessness. I hated gym and sports for I was not agile — a legacy perhaps of a childhood illness — and I tried to get out of lessons and go to the library while my classmates swung over booms, climbed ropes or hung upside-down on the bars.

*St Angela's Uniform
– we always wore Gloves*

On Saturday mornings we had "Degrees", when classes in turn met Mother Mary Angela in the hall for the result of the weekly test to be read out, each girl taking her place, beginning at the top, in a row. However, a Third Degree was read out in front of the whole school and was a punishment far worse than a physical caning. Fortunately, Third Degrees were rarely meted out. After "Degrees", Mother Mary Angela gave us "instruction" on manners or morals. She had the most expressive brown eyes, scintillating when angry but generally speaking so warm and loving.

To change classrooms we walked decorously in pairs from room to room, but more often it was the teachers, nuns or secular, who changed. As the teacher entered, the five minutes' talk allowed between lessons stopped abruptly and we stood.

It all sounds frightfully regimented but was in fact a very happy place. Discipline was expected and accepted and in that framework we worked and played. Contrary to common expectation at that time, no pressure was put upon non-Catholics to accept Catholicism, though we loved singing "Ave Maria" or "Star of the Sea", on sunny mornings in May. Learning the catechism widened my horizon at a time when the gulf between Catholicism and Church of England was immeasurably wider than at the present day. It was also an easy way to have at least one A Plus in my weekly report by learning a couple of answers. Each subject had a page in these report books, filled in weekly by the teachers and taken home to be signed by a parent. We also had a weekly exam, in subjects in rotation, and as a result were assigned our position in class. A few bad results and a pupil was demoted to the B class.

My journey to school involved two tram rides, but during the General Strike of 1926 I wobbled to school across the Flats on my aunt's ancient upright bicycle. This was the prelude to a shiny new model: a Raleigh All Steel which cost the enormous sum of twelve pounds, of which six were saved from birthday and Christmas presents and six paid by my mother. Later it travelled to college with me and finally to the new life on the farm until the acquisition of my first upright Baby Austin.

In the Upper Fifth matriculation was our goal. It was a case of passing in all subjects or of failing completely and taking the whole lot again. Finally came the day when we rode home on the tram with sets of red-bound classics with gilt lettering, a bitter-sweet ending to school days.

CHAPTER THREE

Crays Hill

CHILDHOOD DAYS tend to be recalled as unending summer, but the sound of rain pattering on a roof transports me to wet days spent in the railway carriage in which we enjoyed our holidays. When the rains came, I sat cross-legged on the bed and brought out my three celluloid dolls and a paper bag full of scraps of silk, cotton and linen with which to make sets of clothes. Dresses had matching knickers and petticoats edged with lace and flannel vests completed the outfits. Plaited rafia could be stitched to make an elegant hat for the biggest doll — just six inches tall — with blue ribbons hanging down at the back. These ribbons fulfilled a longing hidden since the day when cousin Joyce and I were bridesmaids. Both wore white silk dresses embroidered with blue, but Joyce had a white hat trimmed with just such blue ribbons while I had only a wide-brimmed leghorn straw — doubtless very expensive — with an enormous satin bow in front. So my doll had blue ribbons. I never made dolls' clothes on sunny days; there was too much to do outside.

Our Victorian grandparents, the Jamiesons, were unusual in their choice of a holiday home. I have often heard how Grandpa, in straw boater and dark grey suit with trousers tightened with bicycle clips, Ethel, my mother, and her sister Violet, in long skirts and blouses with leg-of-mutton sleeves, and their brother Jim in knee-breeches and cap, would set off on their upright bicycles for a day's ride, equipped with carbide lamps in case darkness should overtake them.

It happened that on one trip, undertaken only by Grandpa and his schoolboy son, they were caught in such a deluge that the roads were flooded and they were obliged to spend the night in an inn in the county town of Wickford in Essex, thirty-odd miles from home. Next morning they were following a higher road when Grandpa stopped. "Plots for Sale", read Jim. "I'm going to buy one," replied his father and they turned round and rode back to Wickford to clinch the deal.

"Father knew that railway carriages were for sale," continued my Uncle Jim, then well in his eighties as he re-told the old story, "so while he was at work, mother and I went to Stratford station. Mother hated crossing the railway lines at that busy junction to inspect the carriages. Only one was available, about to be broken up, so she took it, with its doors marked '3rd. G.E.R. (Great Eastern Railway) 593'.

"The carriage was taken by rail to Wickford station," the story continued, "and then the fun began. On a wet day it was loaded on to a dray pulled by four horses and hauled three miles to Crays Hill.

"Just as it arrived," he went on, "there was a regular downpour. How those horses pulled the dray over the sodden ground I'll never know. Somehow the carriage was slid on its side down the ramp and then, with ropes and piled-up sleepers, was raised without a single window being broken," marvelled the old man. "But it was not straight and to this day stands at an angle across the width of the ground."

The carriage being in position, those Victorians started to furnish it. Since Grandpa was a silversmith there were only weekends and Bank Holidays, apart from the annual week's holiday, in which to achieve this purpose.

In those days, railway carriages had comfortably shaped, low-backed, wooden seats with a high wall at intervals to divide the compartments. Two spring mattresses were laid across the wooden seats of one compartment for the women folk and in the smaller compartment a mattress was placed for the men with a crosswise bed at the foot later, to accommodate Nicholas.

But all this happened before my mother was married. The family have often recounted how Grandma and Grandpa with their four children took the train to Laindon Station and then set out to walk the $4\frac{1}{2}$ miles to Crays Hill.

"Each time, we took a few more things down in our dress baskets," Grandma used to tell me. Those wicker dress

The Railway Carriage at Crays Hill

baskets with top fitting over the bottom enclosed by a leather "harness" grew heavier and heavier as they trudged on and on towards Crays Hill. Even then, the walking was not over for teenage Jim and Gertrude. They had to walk the mile down Church Hill to Gower's Farm to fetch the milk. On the way back they were allowed to sit under the "half-way" tree and have a drink from a small mug carried in Jim's pocket.

However difficult the beginnings, by the time we children were born, the carriage was a comfortable holiday home equipped with the necessities of life and loved by all members of the family. The excitement of waiting to set off for Crays Hill was almost unbearable. Grandma, always ready ahead of time, sat with her mushroom straw hat and grey coat on, green and white sunshade in hand, with the black bag hanging from her arm. This "black bag" took the place of a handbag. When one showed signs of wear, Grandma would make another from black serge lined with the remains of some worn out garment, closed with draw strings of black cord. At last the moment to set out arrived: first a walk across Wanstead Flats to Manor Park station. Then the hustle and bustle of Liverpool Street station where we met Grandpa and, to crown the journey, there was Miss Gower at Laindon station waiting with her horse and trap. Riding high above the countryside waving to all whom we passed — this was joy indeed.

Arriving at the top of Crays Hill we ran joyfully up the cinder path, flanked by meadows of buttercups, daisies and marguerites. Then, a breathless wait at the small wooden gate under the silver poplar tree, gazing at the carriage slumbering behind the green casement curtains, till the elders arrived more leisurely and Grandpa unlocked the padlock. We were there!

On arrival, Grandpa's first job was to put up the flag, and once the Union Jack was flying over the water butt we were really "in residence". While Grandma lit the old-fashioned round Rippingale oil stove to boil water, fetched in a watering can from a farm nearby, in the black iron kettle, Nicholas and I rummaged in the tin trunk for our treasures. Here were rag doll, Betty, Soldier Boy, two tennis rackets and a ball, a cricket bat and ball, two small, shiny, brown teapots for gypsy picnics when Marie biscuits soaked in water made the most exotic imaginary dishes — and finally, the shot-gun which Nicholas lovingly fingered, but was allowed to use only under Grandpa's supervision.

Grandpa soon set to work cutting the high grass with a long, two-handled scythe. Nicholas and I "made the hay" by tossing it around, rolling and tumbling in the sweet smelling stuff, getting it caught in hair and clothes. Each morning, when the dew had dried, Grandma made a tour of inspection, sniffing a handful and rubbing it between her fingers. When it was pronounced fit, the hay quilts which covered the beds were emptied of last year's contents and stuffed afresh. If you have never slept beneath a freshly filled hay-quilt, one of life's joys has passed you by.

Trees were important at Crays Hill. I was fortunate in sleeping next to the carriage windows and whenever I hear the wind whispering in Lombardy poplars, I am carried in spirit to quiet summer evenings in "the haunted air of twilight" as I lay watching the gentle movement of the leaves. There was the silver poplar too, casting a spreading shade where, on sunny afternoons, one carried deck-chairs and books which were often abandoned to the delight of watching the blue sky between the silver leaves.

One particularly hot summer we wore bathing costumes and, when the heat became unbearable on the south side of the carriage, a few steps round to the other side, passing the fragrant Gloire de Dijon rose bush on the way, brought one into the unbelievable coldness of the carriage's shadow.

During this heatwave Nicholas and I slept out of doors on camp beds. Covered with yellow horse-rugs, striped red and black at each end, and a hay quilt, we were deliciously warm. We watched the first stars appear above the poplar trees and drifted to sleep in the fragrance of the large white roses gleaming from the tall bush at our feet.

Nicholas and I spent most of our summer holidays with Grandma and Grandpa at the carriage, while my mother, with her brother and sister travelled by train to Wickford at midday on Saturday — banks and offices were open on Saturday mornings in those days. On Fridays, therefore, we walked down the hill with Grandma to the wooden lathe store, for the week's shopping. Here, Mr Gower weighed sugar with a scoop into blue sugar-paper bags, and cut butter from a huge slab and patted it into shape with ribbed, wooden butterpats. Cheese from a nearby farm was cut into wedges by a wire, while rice and tea, dried prunes and tapioca were weighed into paper bags. Biscuits were sold loose from a tempting display of 7lb tins arranged at an angle in a frame in front of the counter. As the tins were emptied, broken pieces were left at the bottom and for twopence (less than 1p), half a pound of delicious morsels could be bought to be spread out at the carriage, meticulously shared by us children, and eaten slowly to savour each delicious crumb, especially of our favourite mixed creams.

While the groceries were being purchased we prowled around the Aladdin's cave which was the general side of the shop. There anything from boot buttons to paraffin, rope to writing paper could be bought, presided over by Mrs Gower, tall and thin with an extremely high-pitched voice. Admittedly, this lady very often could not "lay her hand" on a bottle of ink, or plimsolls of the required size, but shopping was a leisurely business and at last she would emerge, dishevelled, with a triumphant squeak "He-re we-e ar-e!", while the boxes with spilled contents disturbed in the search, added to the disorder in marked contrast to Mr Gower's meticulous arrangement of the groceries.

The main business of shopping done, Grandma sailed across the road to the post office to buy some halfpenny stamps and for her usual chat with stout Mrs Hemmings. We stood outside the shop window discussing the serious business of spending our Saturday twopence. For this sum we could buy eight separate sweets, chosen from sherbet dips, liquorice laces, toffee bars, humbugs (two for a farthing), a twist of pear drops, acid drops, aniseed balls or a twisted barley sugar stick — unless we decided to launch out and buy a halfpenny bar of chocolate. The sweets lasted us the weekend. There would be no more until the next Saturday.

Soon after midday on Saturday, Grandma began to cook on the oil stove, the steak, delivered by Mr Franklin, the butcher from Wickford, the previous evening, while we went to meet our mother, aunt and uncle on their $2\frac{1}{2}$ mile walk from Wickford station. We were all ravenous by the time we reached the carriage and the smell of steak frying was the most delicious in the world. On fine days we ate out of doors, and washed up in rainwater on a wooden bench on a platform of sleepers.

Once a month, my aunt would produce the magazine *Little Folks* and I slipped away with my treasure to the oak tree at the end of "the ground", where a convenient bough formed our secret place. Here among the leaves I read the serious articles first, leaving the delight of short stories and the serials to the end. My mother had the magazines bound annually as birthday presents. Turning the pages sixty years later, they are still full of interest: Little Folks Library Club, Little Folks Nature Club, Pets and Pastimes, and well-loved characters from serials by May Wynne and Elsie Oxenham, leap from the stories to demand that their adventures be re-read.

Our mother would quietly give us a few sweets or some little present. I wonder whether those weekends were really happy for her. She had an interior life of her own with a deep love of learning and reading, but, being a widow, she was trapped by kindness since Grandmother took over the care of the children while mother worked to support us. Surrounded by her mother and father, brother and sisters, she must have longed sometimes to have her children to herself. Even the decision to cut off my auburn curls was made by my aunts, since they were "taking my strength". The reward of a wide, pale blue satin ribbon for my bobbed hair did not compensate for the loss of my curls which I vainly tried to sew on to my rag doll's head.

On Sunday mornings the family trooped down the hill to the church, which was a mile down a side road opposite the wooden shop. Strangely, I remember only sunny Sunday mornings, never macs and galoshes.

Punctually at two minutes before 11 a.m. the squire's trap drew up at the church door. The squire's lady entered, nodding kindly to Grandma, followed by the squire and his sons, and the service began. The singing was whole-hearted if a trifle dissonant. In the choir of three, Mrs Gower's high treble dominated and she often had the organist at the harmonium puffing as he treadled to keep up with her. Minnie was deaf and sang off-key, but Mabel, her sister, had a good contralto voice. We in the congregation sang the old favourites lustily in our own time. The prayer for the parish to "restoo-oore the penitent, rec-ov-er the fallen" is immediately linked with the open door opposite our pew, with the hens from the nearby farm pecking in the grass, the buzz of a bee and always the birds singing in the woods behind the church.

After the service there was a general exchange of news and much shaking of hands with "welcome back" from the congregation. The squire's trap was brought round and the pony trotted off even farther "down the hill". It was our particular delight on the way home, to run along the white-painted bridge at the side of the road, so placed for use when the "wash" was flooded in winter.

It is sometimes difficult to think how the time was passed in those days before the advent of wireless — let alone television — but at Crays Hill, life was simple. If fine, we stayed out of doors until bedtime, playing with the local children, Vivian and Muriel and their brother. In pairs we galloped across Taylor's field with a harness of skipping rope and played bat and ball. Sometimes the family walked through fields deep in marguerites to Mr Benson's for eggs and tomatoes. On the way back in June time, we watched, fascinated, as the traction engines standing at either end, pulled the mowing machine to and fro across the field, leaving flat swathes of fragrant grass to scent the evening air.

On wet evenings, Grandpa reached beneath the wooden seat for his fiddle and we chose songs in turn as the rain pattered on the roof. Then, after a cup of cocoa, I ran along the sleepers into the next compartment to bed, hoping that enough light remained for a read. Punctually at 10 o'clock, through the wooden wall, one heard, "A little drop of hot, Pem?" and then the chink of glasses. What "hot" was we had not a clue in those days.

Outside the front of the carriage grew a bush of Old Man (called in Somerset, Lad's Love), deliciously fragrant when crushed between the fingers. A whiff of the pungent scent sixty years later recreates the magic of summer days, buttercup gold fields, hay quilts, rain pattering on the carriage roof, steak frying on an oil stove, pink rose patterned cups and a row of paperbacked books on a wooden shelf. Here *A Welsh Singer* rubbed shoulders with *Scarlet Pimpernel*, and with *Beau Brocade*, *Life's Trivial Round*, *A Peep Behind the Scenes* and *Christy's Old Organ* were read and re-read each summer.

It is all different now, I am told. The cinder path is a tarmacked road lined with neat bungalows built in the buttercup and daisy field. The Lombardy poplars remain and the silver poplar guards the patch of waist-high grass and bramble, where once the carriage stood.

CHAPTER FOUR

College and Early Teaching Days

MY EIGHTEENTH was the most miserable of all my birthdays. Sitting on the white bench at the end of the hall at St Angela's, waiting for morning assembly, I felt suddenly incredibly old. The future, so casually planned fell in splinters at my feet: the final year in the Upper Sixth, followed by a three year degree course in French at London University and a further year's teaching training would make me twenty-four, and not a penny earned. Clear as a flash I saw that it was not fair to ask my mother to support me for another five years on her widow's pension. At that age, many girls were thinking of marriage. But what to do? The Civil Service like my mother? But I was not good at figures. That offer from my uncle's friend of a job at Marshall & Snelgrove's in Oxford Street? I turned from the thought in despair. A lifetime of selling clothes in a stifling department store. I wasn't interested in clothes.

"That girl ought to be out earning," I'd heard my Grandfather say. It was true. The day was spent in mental ferment. Only one thing was clear. The happy, sheltered life at St Angela's would be over in a few months.

Perhaps it was not chance and not pure coincidence that when I wandered restlessly into the garden on that January afternoon, as dusk was falling our next door neighbour was taking her washing from the line.

"What's the matter, girl? You look as gloomy as the weather," she said and, thankful for someone to talk to, I told her of my doubts.

Characteristically, Mrs C. took charge. "What *you* want to do is primary teaching, girl," she said. "Come in after tea."

Of course! Young children! I loved youngsters. Why hadn't

I thought of it before? With a surge of relief I prepared tea before my mother returned from one of her visits to the sick or lonely.

In a week's time, Mrs C. announced that she had contacted her former college at Hockerill on the borders of Herts and Essex. Yes, there was a vacancy caused by a cancellation — here was the address — I was to go for interview the following week — Mrs C. would accompany me — I should start in September. And so one of the most important steps of my life was planned in a whirlwind and in a few short months I set off, by train, for an unknown world.

The very first evening those of us who had not done pupil teaching while waiting for a place — how fortunate I had been! — were directed to the Quad. There hung lists of the schools which we would be attending the following morning to start our first school practice. Desperately lonely, I found my name by that of Miss M., so Joan (as I will call her) and I were thrown together into the whirlpool of teaching, neither having any idea how to start. I am grateful for that apparently haphazard grouping: totally different in character and outlook, we embarked on a lifetime's friendship.

Hockerill College was over a hundred years old, built of mellow stone with beautiful twisted chimneys, the only source of heating being the open fire. For the first year we slept in cubicles with a curtain at the entrance, each containing a bed, some drawers, and pegs for hanging clothes. Water had to be carried and baths were on rota. A prefect slept in the end cubicle. She put lights out at 9.50 p.m. and at 6.45 a.m. a maid clanged the rising bell as she paraded the dormitories. Chapel, which all students attended, was held before breakfast.

During our second year, Joan and I shared East Room, divided by a curtain. It was bitterly cold there. I had the worst chilblains of my life, which my mother cured during half term by soaking my hands in warm water and rubbing them with olive oil. After that, I wore gloves indoors all the time. We had to keep our rooms clean and I remember some soft, home-made polish with a horrid smell and a kind of polisher for the wooden floor. Not long after we left the first study bedrooms were built, today a commonplace, but marvellous in our eyes.

But I enjoyed the life, with its full programme of study and the use of an excellent library to compensate for the hardships.

It seems odd today that no boyfriends were allowed, that stockings had to be worn at all times and that we had to sign in at week-ends by 8.30 p.m. On weekdays, mornings and evenings were time-tabled for lectures, but the afternoons were free for games or walking: an hour's fresh air was obligatory. During the second year I took my bicycle and explored the surrounding countryside, usually scraping in just in time to take my seat for tea beside the anxious Joan. I do not remember having cake, but on Thursday we had currant buns for tea! Food was plain but filling, particularly the steamed and boiled puddings known irreverently as John the Baptist's head and dead baby. Supper was cocoa with bread and pork dripping.

I went to Joan's home for a week-end, having first presented written permission from my mother, and was amazed at the orderliness and precision of everything, with no speck of dust around! Mrs M. would stand at the window, serving-spoon in hand to watch for her husband to appear down the road. Then, as he sat at the table, his meal was placed before him. This miracle of timing never ceased to amaze me. It was the first time I had stayed in a home "with a father" and it was fascinating to see the interplay of relationship between father, mother and daughter. Joan received a warm, but far less ordered welcome in our home — a complete change for her too!

College days over, we were thrown out into the harsh reality of searching for jobs, which were difficult to find in 1931. Here again, thanks to the help of our neighbour Mr C., himself a headmaster, I was appointed to a junior school, though I had hoped for an infants' posting.

During those early years most of one's effort was expended on keeping order. We still had stepped classrooms with double desks fixed to the floor. At home time the routine was: "Stand! Hands together! Eyes closed! 'Now the day is over' (sung in various keys). Good afternoon children. Good afternoon, Madam," and the march in lines to the cloakroom. This was at the behest of the headmistress, whose main job seemed to be to prowl round to ensure that "order" was maintained, and that no buzz of conversation issued from the classrooms. It was a nightmare at times. My first experience was of a C class, needing individual attention. How to give this while keeping the other children absolutely quiet was a mystery beyond my comprehension. Class demonstration of "sums" was the method of the day and then exercises were set. The brighter ones finished the task and became restless, so stragglers simply fell by the wayside. At college my training had been almost entirely in infant work involving far more freedom for the children, and I felt ill-equipped for this regimented block teaching which the seven elderly teachers achieved with ease. I had one contemporary, taking the A class, who devised a simple expedient. When I tried to discuss our work she said, "Give the dull ones poetry to write out! I do!" She got good "results" with the top group and never seemed to notice the rest. She was always hatted and coated, ready to walk out with her class at home time; I always had things to put away and marking to do or to take home.

Registers were a nightmare, for an error or alteration was a serious offence. "You could lose your job for this," I was once told by the headmistress when summoned to her sanctum down some stairs from the hall, to explain how I had come to mark an absent child present. Biros were unknown. We had bottles of red and black ink and steel nibbed pens. Erasions were impossible and there was the constant fear of a bottle of ink being upset over the precious document. Marked with red dashes, registers had to be closed with black noughts at 9.30a.m., precisely at the end of the statutory scripture lesson, and at exactly 2.10p.m. in the afternoon. It was difficult to remember to break off a lesson and attend to this duty at the correct moment. Managers called frequently to inspect the registers, and, of course, the figures had to be balanced at the end of every term. All this stemmed from the days, then not so long past, when teachers were paid by attendance and results.

We were issued with stock once a month when all requirements for the following four weeks had to be written in the stock book and presented to the headmistress. Forget something and the children had to go without. One had to be careful too, about ordering. "I see you had a box of nibs last month," I was told, "and what happened to the pencils issued the previous month?"

Since pen and ink were used from seven years old, work was frequently smudged despite the issue of squares of blotting paper for each exercise book, and who could help dropping an occasional drop of ink? But once I scored a triumph. The headmistress set the arithmetic examination papers and marked them herself. I was in despair. The class and I were sure to get a scolding. She came in. "These results not very good," she began, but," and she actually smiled, "they are the neatest set of papers in the school. I only found one small blot." Smiles rippled round the room and I basked in that crumb of praise which so rarely came the way of a junior teacher.

One dinner hour during those early years, I arrived home to find my French pen-friend, who was staying in London, by our fireside. "Could she come to school with me in the afternoon?" she asked. I was worried. How did one occupy forty children while chatting to a vivacious young Frenchwoman? The first period for the afternoon was an "observation" lesson on butterflies, I think. The plan of the lesson was for the teacher to hold forth for fifteen or twenty minutes on the given subject and then for the children to read the relevant chapter round the class, good readers and those who could barely stumble through a paragraph alike. Incredibly boring for the children — and for a visitor — and desperately hard for the teacher to keep up their attention. What did those children know about butterflies? Their houses had backyards instead of gardens and Wanstead Park was a long tram ride away.

The days of nature tables, on which caterpillars weave their cocoons, when suddenly someone spots a butterfly emerging, and formal work is abandoned until the miracle is achieved and we all troop into the playground to watch it fly away, were years away in the future. At the very least, they would have made the room untidy, and how could children arrange their specimens or look for the name of a wild flower in a reference book when they were chained to their desks all day?

To return to Suzy's visit. I suspect that, greatly daring, I changed the timetable and set the class to write a composition, that great stand-by. To have had them clustering round a young French visitor asking questions and learning something about France in the most natural way, would have been impossible. There would have been a noise! However, out of that visit came one small innovation. After spending my summer holiday at Suzy's home at the foot of the Cevennes in the Rhône Valley, I set up a small museum of objects and photographs of the ancient town of Tournon, nestling among the vine-covered slopes and of ancient farmhouses and farming methods high in the Cevennes. Then I read *Travels With a Donkey*, to the children. My effort was noted and approved.

Shortly after Suzy's visit, one of my colleagues was absent from school and asked her father to deliver a note to my mother for me to take to school in the afternoon (we did not have the 'phone in ordinary houses then). My mother was busy frying sausages for my dinner and suddenly remembered that she had promised to go round to her mother's. When Mr B knocked at the door he was asked in. "Would you mind very much looking after these sausages for ten minutes while I slip round to mother's?" she asked her surprised visitor, and he, to his amazement, found himself with a frying pan in his hand until my mother came running back!

Our junior girls' school was on the floor above the junior boys. Traipsing up and down those stairs with monitors posted on landings to report talkers was no joke, and "drill" lessons became a nightmare. After being kept at their desks for so long, the children tended to go wild and it was terribly difficult to get the faultless "lines" required for the performance of set exercises in the 1922 Syllabus which we were still using. "Trunk forward be---e--end!" shrilled the teacher's voice, or "Feet apart---jump!" or perhaps "Arms fling! One, two, one, two." Finally, "Hands on hips! Heels raise! Knees full be---end! Straighten those backs! Knees stretch! Heels lower!" After this exhilarating exercise, the children must be marshalled upstairs and put back to work.

The 1933 syllabus gave a variety of movements in each group of body exercises for arms, trunk, head etc. but did allow a "break" between each group such as star-jump or "on the spot run!" The whole session opened with an "activity" extremely difficult to control. Before each lesson a selection of exercises must be learnt, and often a young teacher glanced surreptitiously at a scrap of paper clutched in the hand for fear of missing an exercise. On wet days, drill must be conducted in the hall, surrounded by classrooms, within hearing range of the head, in theory without noise. Few children had plimsolls but a concession to exercise might be made by the removal of a top jersey. One elderly teacher could remember the days when children were literally sewn into their clothes for the winter.

In September many of the families departed to Kent for two weeks "'opping". The whole family picked hops and in sunny years returned bronzed from their camping in the open air. We had gypsies in our classes sometimes and though their attainment was poor, owing to inadequate schooling, they were happy children with their long colourful skirts and hair in tiny braids. I specially remember Gentilia. When the nurse came round at monthly intervals, the order was "heads on desks" while she searched for livestock in the hair; there was never a dirty-haired gypsy to my remembrance. Other children were sent home designated "one" or "two" according to the treatment required before being re-admitted to school.

We did pastel drawings, in tissue-lined books, of an object set up by the teacher. It was remarkable how an apple would have a highlight in exactly the same spot wherever a child was sitting, placed in accordance with the teacher's instructions.

There were still three, hour-long needlework lessons just as when I was a pupil, with the same tacking, running and hemming practice, and knitting was taught. The top classes learnt to knit on four needles ready for making socks and gloves in the senior school. Teaching knitting to left-handed children was like a Chinese puzzle with "madam", as we were called, in as much of a tangle as was the child.

Occasionally, a child from another class would enter, having knocked of course, and wordlessly hand a ruler to the teacher. There was an inspector on the premises! Immediate panic set in, communicating itself to the children, making them restless and harder to control. As the door opened, a young teacher's heart beat furiously: one faltered, stumbled and dried up completely giving the impression, no doubt, of complete incompetence. Inspectors must have realised that this was a hang-over passed on to us by the older generation of teachers, from the days when teachers were paid by results. The dread of inspectors persisted till, in later years, confidence in one's work increased and they no longer appeared as ogres intent on pulling a victim to pieces.

Once a month "one bell" was rung, and all teachers went to the hall to receive and count their pay packets under the watchful eye of the guard who escorted the carrier of so much wealth from school to school. My first month's salary amounted to twelve pounds, sixteen shillings and sixpence, for East Ham

*My Mother, my Brother and Myself
at Walton-on-the-Naze*

was one of the better paid boroughs. I always bought Grandma a box of Cremona toffee for three shillings on the way home on pay day, gave my mother two pounds for the month, and the rest was divided into little tins between clothes, holidays, travel to school, savings and insurance. There was not much to spend! But in those days a good summer dress cost twelve and elevenpence (65p) and a pair of shoes about the same, while a week's holiday board and lodging at the seaside could be had for two pounds ten shillings at a superior guest house.

So the first few years passed uneventfully. Four times a day I rocked for twenty minutes in a tram, always with a book to read. Fortunately the conductors came to know the destination of their "regulars" or I might have landed up in Woolwich Docks, absorbed in my reading, had they not shouted "Vicarage Lane! Vicarage Lane!" or given me a gentle shake.

No married woman was employed as a teacher in the 'thirties and we were under a moral, if not a written, obligation to teach for three years after training, so that marriage was out of the question. Boyfriends were for fun and dancing, for the "pictures" and tennis in those early days.

Suddenly a cloud swooped across the horizon. War was imminent. We were to be evacuated with our classes to safe areas in the country.

CHAPTER FIVE

Evacuation

THERE WAS furious activity in the school as we prepared for evacuation. We were all issued with gas masks and instructed in their use, wearing them for a few minutes at a time at first then for longer periods. The masks, we were told, must be carried with us at all times, and this brought the horror of war infinitely nearer.

Parents had to make the heart-breaking decision as to whether to send their children away or to risk the expected bombing. Teachers had no choice. Rucksacks were packed and re-packed with essential clothes and I had the additional burden of the first aid kit, fervently hoping that no one would need attention on the journey.

On September 1st, 1939, a crocodile of 290 children from the junior boys' and girls' school wound its way to East Ham station flanked by anxious parents. Nicholas had already left with his insurance firm for "somewhere in the country" and my mother was left to solitary endurance. We had made pitiful attempts to ensure her safety: thick curtains hung at windows which were criss-crossed with strips of sticky music-mending paper to prevent splintering when the bombs fell; in the cellar was a deck chair and a meagre supply of tinned food and a tin-opener. No one knew what horror lay ahead and the whole future was filled with dread. I waved her goodbye, a brave, lonely figure standing at the gate of "116" wondering when — or if — we would meet again?

At East Ham station we settled the children in the train, lonely, bewildered and tearful. At Paddington we were ushered into a main-line train still without a clue as to where we were going, until, about an hour after the commencement of the journey, a friendly guard disclosed that we were bound for Axbridge in Somerset. None of us had heard of the place. The journey, though long, was uninterrupted by stops and in the early afternoon the guard said we were nearing our destination. However, we steamed through Axbridge and stopped at Cheddar station.

The bedraggled party, clutching bags and gas masks were met by half the population of Cheddar and escorted through the village, led by J. J. Tyson, the local headmaster, to the Methodist Hall for a cup of tea. As I sipped the hot sweet brew I saw, pinned to the wall, an illuminated text, "Fear not, little Flock" and felt comforted.

Then began the distribution of children to the families who had agreed to take them. Girls were easy to place, and some would take a brother and sister, but boys were a problem and it was dusk before the last child had found a home. Then it was the teachers' turn. I was whisked off to the corner shop where an elderly lady who was 82 or 92, "I do forget, my dear" she told me, lived with her daughter who kept the draper's shop. They did not really want to take anyone into their orderly, routine-run home, but with a little persuasion I was taken for the agreed adult rate of £1 weekly!

Having got over their fear of a "foreigner" in their home, these dear people were kindness itself, and the least I could do was to settle into their routine as far as possible. Being fearful of fire, the grate was raked out at 8.15p.m. each evening after our cup of cocoa, so that no spark remained when we processed to bed at 9p.m. after the five locks on the outer doors had been bolted. I was puzzled by this attention to security, not knowing till long afterwards that the family's worldly wealth was contained in a safe hidden behind a high backed chair in the sitting room. Banks were not to be trusted I was told, they could break at any moment. So when payment had to be made for shop goods a covering amount was deposited in the bank so that the cheque could be written.

We had no blackout at the upstairs windows so I presume we undressed in the dark! Fortunately I had a good torch by which to read beneath the bedclothes.

The corner shop dealt in haberdashery and essential items of clothing. It was a thrill when the crates of stock arrived to help to sort out the goods — all marked "Utility" of course.

Clothing coupons did not stretch far: each purchase had to be weighed carefully against coupon value. I knitted many jumpers with wool costing $4\frac{3}{4}$d. an ounce — just 2p. — which washed and wore for years. One did not buy jerseys in those days.

From Mrs Pavey I learnt much of old country ways as she told me stories of her life in Cheddar. She had never travelled farther than to Weston-super-Mare for a day's outing, when, as a child, she had gone in a horse-drawn brake once a year.

"We girls," she told me, "dressed in our best, used to walk a mile along the road to meet the brake in order to have a longer ride". They always stopped halfway at Banwell for the horse to be watered while the men repaired to the local inn. At Banwell there is still a mounting block from the days when the horse was the main means of transport.

I learnt some Somerset words too. "The stones do 'eave'", Mrs P would say, when, on a warm, overcast day the kitchen flagstones became wet with condensation. I heard for the first time of "lammergers" (corpses) and how her father used to mend "shards" in the limestone walls which run up and down the Mendip Hills. She told me, too, how the Cheddar cheese used to be made: each farmer, or anyone owning a cow, contributing his milk until he was entitled to take away a cheese.

During those early war days I put on a stone in weight. Hanging in the outhouse was a side of the most delicious home-cured bacon with bristly rind. A couple of slices of this each morning with fried potatoes was my regular breakfast — which I loved — and for dessert we always had apple pie. "We must eat up the apples from the orchard," Mrs P explained, so a fresh pie was baked every Saturday and Wednesday. I reckoned that I ate thirty-nine pies in all during the first year with a *very* occasional break for a trifle on Sunday.

Miss P. and I became great friends despite the gap of thirty years in our ages. We experimented with dressmaking together, and even ventured out into the blackout on little excursions to the newly opened cinema a couple of hundred yards along the road, and once even to a whist drive and dance at the Cliff Hotel — but more of that later.

In free time I wandered among the anemone fields where strawberry growing had been suspended for the duration. Surprisingly the flower trade flourished, and I was often allowed to pick bunches of the long-stemmed red, purple, pink and white flowers to send home to my mother.

Once a month we had washing day, which involved sorting piles of "whites" and "coloureds" overnight, setting the whites to soak and getting up at crack of dawn to light the fire under the copper and get breakfast over before the washerwoman arrived. This lady spent the whole day washing, wringing with the heavy wooden-rollered mangle, including blueing and starching and hanging out, all for five shillings (25p.) and a dinner. During the evening we pulled the sheets and folded piles of clothes for the following day's ironing. Then came the mending. To save coupons we refurbished underclothes, fashioning ways of doing without elastic, which was scarcely ever to be had, and darned our lisle stockings over and over again. Nylons were unknown and one possibly owned one pair of silk stockings "for best".

On weekdays we had to keep the evacuated children occupied. The local school worked from 8a.m. till noon and we took over the building from 1p.m. to 5p.m. In the morning we gathered in the Methodist hall for activities, mostly chanting tables, singing or doing exercises under the direction of teachers in turn. On fine mornings — and fortunately 1940 was a good summer — we took our groups of about twenty children for walks, exploring field and lane.

One glorious morning I did not join forces with another group as usual, but led my charges across a delightful field of buttercups, blithely ignoring the dew. Just before dinner time an irate foster mother arrived at Mrs P's door dragging an unwilling Johnny. "Would I look at his shoes!!!?" They were yellow, with buttercup pollen sticking to the damp leather. I saw her point and Johnny and I wrestled with brush and polish, exchanging a secret smile remembering our happy morning. Poor Johnny had a dim time in that spotless household, fearful of doing anything in case he "made a mess". After that I was careful to carry a duster and return him with polished shoes, rather than keep to the roads. These town children had had little opportunity to roam the fields.

Some children had difficulty in relating to country life. They missed the rough and tumble of street play and the fish and chip shops, the Saturday mornings at the "flicks" for the blood-and-thunder serial in which the hero was left in some desperate situation until the following week. There were others who revelled in the new-found freedom of hillside and stream. Some country foster-parents were appalled at the paucity of their charges' clothing, while some parents who visited their children were horrified at the outward appearance of some of the cottages (although the children lived comfortably within), and took them back to the crowded streets and houses of the London suburbs.

During that period of the "phoney war" when nothing seemed to be happening, many families did drift back to London, often to be re-evacuated when the bombing started. But many firm friendships were forged: some children who remained being adopted or permanently fostered and later marrying local boys. Twenty years after evacuation I was amazed, after an operation, to have the stitches taken out by a Sister who had come from East Ham with us as a child.

At week-ends we were not required to look after the children so two members of the staff and I tramped the Mendips with a sandwich lunch in our pockets and gas masks slung over our shoulders. We formed an unlikely trio — S.B.G., that awe-inspiring figure from the Vicarage school of my early teaching days, uncertificated, but an outstanding teacher. S.B.G. always took the scholarship class, obtaining excellent results and, in fact, one year the top girl in the borough was from her class. Then there was A.D., stocky and round-faced, quiet and serene in manner. We nicknamed her "Rover", for, no matter where we roamed on Mendip, she could be relied on to "sniff out" the way home. Lastly myself, still a raw teacher unsure of myself in many ways and delighted to be accepted as a friend by the other two.

We revelled in those wide open spaces, with the wild, gorse-covered slopes of Blackdown from the top of which, at 1,068 feet, we had marvellous views of the sparkling Bristol Channel and, when rain threatened, of the coast of Wales where factory chimneys smoked. There were patches of white bog cotton warning us to keep away from deep bogs on the old red sandstone and flaming slopes of heather in autumn. Then we picked bilberries and huge, juicy blackberries to take home to make pies. There were rose hips to be harvested too, to be made into the rose hip syrup so widely used in wartime as a source of vitamins. We walked and talked, sat in the sun or braved the wind and rain and loved it all.

Occasionally there was a brief weekend or holiday and I usually managed to get home, partly by train, sometimes by a lift in a car, to spend a few precious hours with my mother and to visit my grandmother. When the bombs began to fall, I joined my mother under the kitchen table. It was better to start the night there than to be awakened by the wailing of the air raid sirens and to be obliged to drag oneself downstairs. On the mantelpiece, just within my view as I lay on the hard floor, was an illuminated card bearing the words of King George VI on his memorable first broadcast:

> I said to the man who stood at the gate of the year, "Give me a light that I may see," and he replied, "Put your hand into the hand of God; that shall be better than a light and safer than a known way."

It helped.

One February day in 1940, S.B.G., Rover and I, walked to Charterhouse on Mendip in search of snowdrops. These, we were told, grew on patches that were once the gardens of cottages long since disappeared.

Up Cheddar Gorge we tramped, magnificent in winter solitude, with cliffs towering to 480 feet on the right-hand and sloping gently on the left. Gradually the gradient evened out somewhat and the slopes on either side were covered with tussocky grass and outcrops of limestone. About a mile and a half up the Gorge, we climbed a stile beside a five-barred gate and followed the track to Velvet Bottom, passing Black Rock Quarry, by then disused. A mile or so up the grassy Bottom a gate opened into Longwood. We followed the winding path in single file between steep slopes covered with trees, mainly beeches still bearing russet-brown leaves. An occasional rabbit scurried across the path, a robin sang, but otherwise all was stillness.

From the wood we emerged into a farmyard and passed the end of a farmhouse where we were fascinated to see a pink (though we, in our town ignorance, called it red!) hunting coat hanging to air. A farmer came down the yard as we stopped to admire the coat, with a lamb across his shoulders. "That's my brother's," he said. "Here he comes." The brother emerged from the house and obligingly conducted us round the stables to see the horses on which they had hunted that day.

Feeling that we had had a taste of real country life, we went on our way, little thinking we had just spoken to my future husband outside my future home!

A month or so later, Miss P. suggested that we should go together to a whist drive and dance at the Cliff Hotel. I was not particularly fond of whist but the dance sounded fun, so, dressed in my best green pan-velvet dress with rose pink lining in the upstanding collar, we set off — on foot of course.

During the whist, as we moved around the room, the young farmer of the hunting coat came to my table. After refreshments we danced together and so it all began. Friends said that it was the velvet dress which had attracted him! However, Tom invited me to the first film to be shown in the newly opened cinema at Cheddar — *Goodbye, Mr Chips* — and then for a ride on one of his horses.

(There is a sequel to that evening hidden in the folds of that dress. I loved it, knowing that I looked well in the deep green with my auburn hair and throughout the years it hung in the corner of my wardrobe for purely sentimental reasons. Then, nearing our Ruby wedding, I acquired a long brocade skirt in green, shot with peacock blue. For weeks, shops were searched for a top to go with it but none could provide the exact shade of green. I was reconciling myself gloomily to wearing an old dress when Tom said slowly, "That green velvet you wore the first time we danced together would have been just the job!" It was and, still more surprising, it fitted and would make a splendid top! The wheel had come full circle. We set out together secure in the magic of the green velvet dress.)

When friends and family heard that I intended to be married,

Tom and Myself on horseback

they did their best to dissuade me. S.B.G. was genuinely concerned. "It won't be all riding round on horses," she warned me. "What's more, his mother will lead you the devil of a life," she said.

As to my own mother, she was desperately worried, as I gathered from a letter written on best notepaper, always a sign of something amiss, urging me to talk to my Uncle Harold, a barrister, who later became Sir Harold Saunders on his retirement as chairman of the Patent Office. No wonder she was worried, Here was I planning to live on the top of Mendip, four miles from the nearest village, indeed, two miles from the next farm, sharing a house with my mother-in-law in a life that was completely alien to anything I had experienced. I had left her when I was evacuated to Cheddar with the school children, unwillingly abandoning our mother to her lonely life with Teddy, her little brown dog, and two cats. Even Grandma and Uncle Jim went to their holiday home but this lay in the path of enemy bombers en route for London, so they returned. For ninety-two successive nights of air raid warnings they remained there. Grandma could not go down the cellar steps but compromised by sitting at the top of them beneath the staircase when the siren sounded. Our mother slept alone at "116", under the kitchen table, but one fateful night she undressed and slept behind the piano in the drawing room. That night a "V"-bomb flapped its deadly way, suddenly cut out — a dreaded omen — and dropped on the house opposite.

Mother said afterwards that it was a miracle, with the shattering of her house, the whole front was blown out, that the light in the drawing-room came on, enabling her to find clothes and shoes. Uncle Jim came round at first light and only knew "116" among the rubble by the barking of Teddy, who was trapped by fallen bricks in his wicker chair. He told us later how he had found my mother scraping with her fingers in the ruins of the kitchen, where she actually found the sapphire ring belonging to her sister who had died.

The few pathetic remnants of furniture were stored by the council and our mother had to go and live with Grandma. That was not a happy period. At 82, Grandma was as active and practical as ever, brooking no exception to her well-regulated household management. Mother, while longing to help, even to prepare for Nicholas' brief visits, felt unwanted. If only she could find "a little place" of her own! Then, by a miracle, our mother said, there appeared in a local shop an advertisement for a house to let. Nicholas and I helped to sort out the bits of furniture. During the war furniture was almost impossible to obtain but even the part frame of a chair could be used as a basis for re-making, so gradually the home was built up again.

Perhaps the happiest letter I ever received from my mother was written shortly after the war. "Isn't it lovely!" she wrote,

"I have a job!" The local Homes had begun to split their children into small groups in large houses in the neighbourhood under the care of house mothers and my mother was to do five days a week caring for one of those families. I was a little apprehensive, knowing her lack of "method", but once again she proved, with a definite job which she loved, to be capable and efficient, and now began, I believe, the happiest days of her life. Sadly the council brought in a regulation that women must retire at 65, and my mother who had "let it be understood" that she was in fact ten years younger than was in fact the case, now had to reveal her age of 68 and leave, to her bitter disappointment and the loss to the children in her care.

A couple of years later, the shock of the bomb, the doctor said, began to take its toll and diabetes set in. At "three score years and ten" she was in hospital and hoping to wake in Heaven. But another twelve years of struggle were required of her. Walking at first with one stick, then with two, her indomitable spirit kept on: lonely people still came for a cup of tea and a listening ear and went away with a packet of chocolate from the tin on the dresser.

By now her brother had married, late in life, a Frenchwoman and a Catholic, much to Grandma's chagrin, and the old lady was living alone. But she had her Achilles' heel. Grandma was terrified of lightning and would cover her face with a handkerchief during a storm. What was to be done? Grandma alone in a thunderstorm? My mother got out her wheelchair and pushed it round to Grandma's house. Having found that she could walk with support, it became a daily habit and the bent figure, pushing her chair with a bag on the seat containing brown bread and butter sandwiches, and sugar in case of a threatened insulin coma, became a familiar sight as the seventy-two year-old went to cheer her ninety-year-old mother.

Grandma died at ninety-six. Apart from childbirth she had never had a day in bed in her life. "How could I?" she once said. "I had to look after the family." Although her sight was failing, she still loved to show us the marvel of the centre of a marigold or other flower from the garden, peering through her magnifying glass, and still cut wafer-thin bread with the loaf held close to her breast. Then one Friday she had risen as usual at 7.25 a.m., had "done the soot" and washed the mantelpiece and, sitting talking to her other daughter, our Auntie Vi, Grandma slipped sideways and was gone.

My mother no longer went out but there was still a welcome at "116" for her "odd" friends. She died in St Joseph's Hospice a day or so after Archbishop Heenan had visited her, for he had once been her parish priest. One of the nicest tributes came from her home help. "Your mother found happiness," she said, "in little things."

In his book *The Great Divorce*, C. S. Lewis writes:

". . . and after these a lady in whose honour all this was being done. I cannot now remember whether she was clothed. If she were naked, then it must have been an almost visible penumbra of her courtesy and joy which produced in my memory the illusion of a great shining train that followed her across the happy grass. If she were clothed, then the illusion of nakedness is doubtless due to the clarity with which her inmost spirit shone through the clothes, for clothes in that country are not a disguise; the spiritual body lives along each thread and turns them into living organs. A robe or a crown is as much one of the wearer's features as a lip or eye. Only partly do I remember the beauty of her face."

"Is it . . . is it?" I whispered.

"Not at all," he said. "Her name was Sarah Smith and she lived at Golders Green."

"She seems to be — well, a person of great importance."

"Aye. She is one of the great ones."

"Who are all those young people on each side?"

"They are her sons and daughters. Every young man or boy who met her became her son, even if he was only the boy that brought the meat to her back door. . . ."

"And, hallo! What are all these animals? A cat — dozens of cats, and all those dogs — I can't count them. And the birds and horses!"

"Every beast and bird that came near her had its place in her love. In her they became themselves, and now the abundance of life she has in Christ from the Father flows over into them."

"Yes — It is like when you throw a stone into a pool and the concentric waves spread out farther and farther. Who knows where it will end?"

Those words might have been written about my mother. Looking back, I am amazed that I, always on the timid side, clinging to what I knew, went calmly ahead with the marriage. I realise now that things could have gone very wrong, but, forty years on, I am grateful for those years which followed our marriage in St Gabriel's church at Aldersbrook. My mother-in-law didn't like me. Why should she? A "foreigner" from London, and a teacher at that. However, let it be put on record that before she died, Tom's mother and I were the best of friends.

CHAPTER SIX

Early Farming Days

THE EARLY days as a farmer's wife had a funny side despite their difficulties.

At the wedding I had airily invited Joan to bring her friend Carrie for a farmhouse holiday. Just three weeks later they arrived.

One can imagine the feelings of those two girls, coming from immaculate town houses with every modern convenience, to what must have seemed an impossibly primitive form of living. We were without electricity and our lighting was furnished by two old-fashioned oil lamps. I had really no idea about the use and care of oil lamps, the daily filling and trimming of wicks required, and would cheerfully carry one from room to room, finding it blew out in the draught on the way. Fortunately the days were long — "double summer time" giving farmers longer days for food production — but candles had to be taken to bed, and even for this small light the windows must be blacked out.

Then there was the cooking. At home in London we had had a gas cooker and of course the girls had either gas or electric, but here was I, armed with only a primus and a Rippingill oil stove, with burners on each side of the small oven, with which to cope.

Joan and Carrie hovered at a safe distance from the primus while I, not too expert myself, lit the methylated spirit which flared up. Then at the critical moment, one pumped and hopefully a lovely blue flame appeared round the burner. Pump a little too early and the yellow flame shot up nearly to the ceiling. No wonder we were scared.

Looking back, cooking reminds me of those juggling acts when plates must be kept spinning on rods. First, boil the potatoes on the primus, transfer them to the Rippingwell to keep them boiling. Repeat for a second vegetable. To cook a third vegetable and a steamed pudding was *really* tricky involving one saucepan balanced on another. Horror! The potatoes were off the boil! Transfer them to the primus for a few minutes and repeat with the beans. I remember Joan and Carrie stooping to listen to the Rippingill oven with anxious faces. Was the meat sizzling? Frankly, I do not recall realizing that we ought to be hearing it sizzle. At home, when my mother was unwell, it had been Nicholas who did the cooking.

By the process of keeping things on the boil we managed to get dinner cooked in time for a hungry farmer. I do not remember any real failures. But there was one snag: I usually forgot to put kettles and saucepans of water on the primus and Rippingill to heat for washing-up. It's all very well if brought up to this way of life, but for a Londoner, there was so much to learn.

The mornings were difficult too. The primus must be lit for the early cup of tea and water heated to be carried upstairs in copper jugs for our visitors, accustomed of course to a hot bath every day. On the marble-topped wash-stand stood my mother's green wash bowls with pink roses containing tall jugs of cold water which had to be re-filled daily. We *had* a bath — with running cold water — in the kitchen, covered when not in use. But hot water had to be carried in buckets from the boiler house; not very convenient for visitors!

It was August so we went for walks on Blackdown to pick whortleberries. Unfortunately I did not know of the likelihood of adders lurking in the undergrowth, for none of us had wellingtons. On the return home with purple-stained fingers, I learnt a lot about pastry-making from watching my friends at work making delicious whortleberry pies and tarts.

During that first holiday, Tom drove us to Cheddar to catch the train, on the line long since closed, to the seaside, for a walk along the front: to Weston-super-Mare where the sea was barely visible beyond the vast stretch of mud; once to Burnham, but, best of all, to Clevedon where the sea "while softly moving seemed asleep". That was an idyllic afternoon in the sunshine. Although it was wartime we had a cup of tea in the garden of a café within sight of the sea and, I believe, a cake

Lower Farm, Charterhouse

with it. That was luxury in those rationed days. Then the walk back to the station to catch the little local train to Yatton to change for Cheddar where Tom was waiting.

The shopping was done once weekly in "the shop" in the village, four miles away. Anything forgotten had to be done without, for petrol was too scarce to make the trip more often. But we had advantages too. In those days when the butter ration was 2oz. per person a week, Tom took a little cream daily from the churn and I learnt to make butter by shaking it in a glass jar, later in a wooden churn which must be continuously turned till the change in the slapping sound indicated that the butter had "come". We had eight run-around hens and so could put a *whole* egg in a boil-bake cake made to a fatless recipe when 4oz. of dried fruit was allocated with the rations.

There were vegetables on the farm too: potatoes, swedes (grown for cattle), while turnip tops and cow kale made excellent greens. All materials cost clothing coupons, so Joan, Carrie and I hit on the idea of boiling calf meal bags to whiten them and eradicate the lettering. They then made excellent tea towels, aprons, pillow cases and even, with the help of a dolly dye, cushion covers.

It was a happy time despite the fact that clothes were washed in water boiled on the primus and ironed with a flat-iron heated the same way, when the girls must have missed their Ascot heaters and electric irons. But they entered gamely into the different way of life and there was always so much to talk about; our shared college days and the ever interesting discussion of school life in town and country. Both Joan and Carrie eventually became head teachers, but I was content to remain a class teacher, happy with my own little group rather than with the responsibility of administration.

That kind of holiday could kill or cement a friendship. But they both came again during the war and Joan has visited us every year to the present time when, both being retired, it has become a twice-yearly event in our cottage on the slopes of Mendip.

Joan and Carrie went home leaving me to settle to my new situation. Joan told me much later that she and Carrie had grave doubts as to whether I would be able to carry on in a set-up so alien to my former way of life, under the veiled animosity — to put it lightly — of my mother-in-law who lived in the other half of the farmhouse. But it never occurred to me to give up and go back to London. Difficulties there were: financial setbacks over the death of a cow, and outbreak of husk among the calves or a bad year for crops. Farming without modern mechanical aids, particularly in wartime when we were required to produce as much food as possible, was so vulnerable to weather.

But the very struggle to overcome difficulties brought Tom and me closer together, building a stable relationship which might never have developed had everything been plain sailing. Howard Spring wrote: "As life goes on, I think the proving of love is not so much in enjoying together — Enjoyment may supply the chromium plate but it is the things endured together that provide the bolts and rivets."

In September I returned to school in Cheddar. Tom had to drive me the five miles to the valley and to meet me after school since I could not drive. Soon the autumn was upon us with long dark evenings and the problem of light and heat. We had an open fire in the dining-room, lit at week-ends, but during the week the living-room-cum-kitchen had only the Rippingill cooker for heating. I wondered what it would be like in winter? Then, one day, Tom arrived home with "Joby" — and our problem was solved. "Joby" was a small iron stove standing on attractively curved legs with amazing willingness to light easily and give out warmth in the least possible time. From the moment Tom fixed his long pipe through a hole knocked through the wall, Joby was our friend and comforter. He would burn anything and we could keep a black kettle permanently on his hob, a source of constant hot water. All this for the magnificent sum of two pounds ten shillings!

The problem of light was more difficult to solve. I came from a world of switches by every door and a two-way switch on the stairs, to the yellow flames of the glass-bowled lamps, which now command high prices as antiques, and gave little pools of light in whose orbit one must sit to read or write. (How, I wondered, had Grandma made those exquisite baby gowns with scarcely perceptible stitches?)

The first step forward was provided by Tom's younger sister who gave us a new-fangled Tilley lamp. Hung from the ceiling and pumped at intervals, hissing gently, it shed light from its mantle and seemed to light the whole room, but when I lit it recently during an electricity cut, it gave a very gentle glow!

We still took candles to bed. It is surprising how much light a candle can give and I remembered the words of the childhood hymn: "Jesus bids us shine with a clear pure light, Like a little candle burning in the night."

Tom was used to candles throughout his boyhood. He can remember when they milked by candlelight, small points of light flickering in the eerie darkness in the cow-houses. Candles were lit in the carriage lamps at either side of the trap as the pony trotted several miles to the nearest "local" with Tom's mother or father holding the reins, well wrapped in rugs against the biting cold. An evening in the warmth and comfort of the inn, a cheerful sing-song over a couple of pints, then out into the cold for the trot back home.

Candlelight nowadays is romantic, with its gentle glow, and adds poignancy to the carol service in our neighbouring village on Christmas Eve. The little church at Rowberrow which treasures a fragment of a carved Saxon Cross, is always packed for the candlelit service when evocative memory adds mystery to the crib nestling in greenery on the font. Silver-branched candelabra brought by "the quality" light the chancel, but in the pews each person has brought his own candle in candlestick or jam jar. Fortunately the simple, old-fashioned carols are sung, for modern eyes, used to a blaze of light, find difficulty in reading in the flickering glow. Thoughts may wander, but suddenly the words of the final reading impinge upon the mind," and the Light shineth in darkness and the darkness comprehendeth it not — That was the true light which lighteth every man that cometh into the world."

It is a strange thought that, without darkness, there could be no light, for if light were always around us how would we know it was light? Only man, a reflective creature, can grasp the enormity of the problem of light and darkness. Somewhere here lies the solution to the problem of suffering too deep for our comprehension. Why? We ask. But without sorrow, could we know joy? Without valleys, where would be the mountain tops?

During that first winter at Charterhouse up on Mendip I "saw" the moon for the first time. Tom used to go round the cow-houses before bed to ensure that all was well with the animals and one night I went with him. We stepped outside into the blazing light of the Harvest moon, flooding the world with brilliance such as I had never known in London where the moon was dimmed by street lamps. Every detail of the farmyard was bathed in dazzling light and when the frosts came with the October Hunter's Moon, the stars, red, blue and green far outshone the lights of Piccadilly Circus. It was then that I learnt to follow Orion on his nightly journey across the sky. With the curtains drawn back I could see him from bed and sometimes woke in the early hours to creep into the other bedroom to see how far the great Hunter had travelled during the night.

Stepping back into the warm yellow glow of our Tilley lamp was bewildering, but even here things were happening. It all began with a dynamo which Tom bought from a garage in Cheddar for £4. Then he acquired an old Austin Seven for about the same amount and vanished into a disused stable at the end of the garden.

Hours later he re-appeared, jubilant. "I've done it!" he cried. "Come and see!" I hurried down the garden and there was the belt round the hub of a wheel on the propped-up Austin, and the dynamo was working. Wires began to festoon the walls of the enclosed garden and Tom began to do things with switches indoors, studying a rough diagram drawn for him by a friend, for he knew nothing of electricity. The day we switched on a real electric light was a veritable landmark in our lives. Blackpool had nothing on Lower Farm! As long as the Austin was running we had light. Petrol was a problem, of course, and it was admittedly inconvenient to have to go down the garden to turn the engine off at bedtime — making sure that the candles had been lit — but it was worth it.

From that small start we graduated to a lighting set with storage batteries and a Petter engine and finally to mains electricity with such refinements as an electric iron, an electric fire and finally television — but nothing matched the triumph of that first naked bulb in the living-room.

In the year of the Festival of Britain, 1951, Tom came home from market bursting with enthusiasm. He had been told about Rayburn stoves; he had enquired and we were having one. Once Tom decides on such a step events rush on like a river in flood. Our French friend was due to arrive in three weeks' time with two of her children. The Rayburn must be in by then! Miraculously, it was, for Tom has great powers of persuasion. Copper pipes were laid to bath and sink, the gleaming white stove installed and then came the crowning moment, hot water gushing from taps over sink and bath. Our modernisation was complete.

It was during those war years when petrol rationing made it difficult to go far, that Mendip became my favourite spot on earth, as it still is, "the home of my heart" in hail, rain, sunshine and blizzards.

A little below the summit of Blackdown on the south-facing slope, lies the farmhouse, Lower Farm, Charterhouse, built of limestone. The very name of Charterhouse tells the history of the area, for the Carthusian Monks from Witham Friary had a group of lay brothers housed there to look after the sheep on their extensive lands on Mendip. No part of the building remains but in Longwood, at the point where a stream plunges from the shale into the limestone to form deep caves, there is a pool known to local people as Monkspool, the place where fish were kept alive for the use of the monks in the absence of fridges and deep freezers.

At the time of the dissolution of the monasteries the land was sold to Robert May and the house dated from at least that time. Recent discoveries have led to the conclusion that it was originally a longhouse with raftered roof, later ceiled in to make an upper floor. There is a barn nearby called Longhouse to support this theory.

I loved that house with its feeling of history, revealed bit by bit by the finding of such details as a hearth with an ancient beam and inglenook behind the modern tiled fireplace. Beneath the hearth was a stone-lined cavity, neatly closed by a slab of limestone, the hiding place, historians tell us, for treasured possessions in times of trouble. There was a bread oven in the wall too which brought memories back to Tom, for he can remember how, when he was a boy, his mother used to heat a similar oven with burning faggots and rake out the ashes before baking her bread.

When the time came to leave the farmhouse, I shamelessly kept a key about six inches long, and returned to the empty house to roam at will through its thirteen rooms (impossible when my mother-in-law lived in half the house), exploring additions during the centuries. With a packet of sandwiches and a flask of coffee I sat in the deep, sunwarmed window seat overlooking the garden to complete my first published novel, set, of course, in the farmhouse.

The past surrounded one on every walk around the fields where drystone walls invited the search for fossils; brachiopods, gastropods, sometimes corals and the sections of crinoid stems scattered everywhere, laid down some 250 million years ago when Mendip lay under warm, shallow seas.

But when it was bright and sunny it was easier to imagine the Beaker folk who lived in these same fields some 1600 years B.C. Their Henge, a place of worship, survives as an ancient monument known as Gorsey Bigbury. It is a grassy place, shaped as a soup plate with an upturned saucer in the middle. In the enclosing ditch was found a skeleton buried in a crouched position and, in the other side of the ditch, shards of the beakers which identify the period. Wandering around Gorsey Bigbury one November day a fog, or maybe a low cloud, suddenly swirled around. I was completely cut off with no notion of direction or memory as to how I reached home. It was a terrifying experience: I have never felt so alone.

It was in this wind-swept, grey, stone house that the yearning grew to read more deeply, to widen the horizon of the mind. There was more time then: no television or even transistor radio. The wireless set was dependent on a wet battery which needed frequent re-charging. This meant asking the baker to take it to a garage in Blagdon and return it on his next visit — he called three times a week. My bulging bookcases were still in London awaiting transport which was incredibly difficult to arrange in wartime. When hearing of bombs on the capital I feared more for their safety than for any other material thing.

Meanwhile, I found in the newsagent's shop in Cheddar (which did not yet have a library) a dusty copy of the history of the Bible, a paperback whose name I have forgotten. It was a beginning. Then came Millicent. Irish and about my own age, she lived in the Mendip village five miles away. Millicent opened for me "windows on faery seas forlorn".

We enjoyed the same things: picnics on the beach in Ladye Bay in Clevedon with a little solid fuel stove to boil the sixpenny tin kettle for tea; sunny walks along the cliff path towards Portishead with bushes of flaming gorse to the right and the sea shushing gently on the rocks below to the left; or over the wind-swept Mendip hills. It frequently rained on our outings — but who cared when the rain dripped through my succession of second-hand cars? We laughed and went on talking about Proust (of whom I had never heard), discovered the poetry of Gerard Manley Hopkins, devoured *The Stars in their Courses* and *Through Space and Time*, by Sir James Jeans, revealing his theory of the creation of the solar system and the universe. At last I found a source of unending fascination in the reading of Descartes, Pascal, Evelyn Underhill and *The Perennial Philosophy*. The fact that I understood only a fraction of what I read did not matter in comparison with the joy of catching and holding for a blinding moment the essence of a new idea.

One day Millicent said, "Have you heard of Teilhard de Chardin?" We plunged into *The Phenomenon of Man* by this Jesuit priest, scientist and palaeontologist, whose ideas on evolution were too advanced for the Church in the early '50s. Not being allowed to work in his native France he went to China and, while remaining a priest, carried out palaeontological and archaeological work and was involved in the discovery of Peking man in the caves of Chou Kou Tien.

Here was another world to be explored in books. Teilhard de Chardin died on Easter Day in 1955. His work is now recognised and most of his books are in my bookcase.

As we walked we used to discuss the plots of Millicent's current romantic novel and this gave me the idea of trying a novel myself in fulfilment of a childhood dream of being like Jo March in *Little Women*. This favourite character of childhood days had long red curly hair and, best of all, wrote stories!

Suddenly our little world was shattered by the death of Millicent's husband, Padraig, poet and priest. Millicent told me how, on that night long ago in the vicarage on Mendip, when telling our fortunes with cards, she had seen tragedy in his cards and I remembered how abruptly she had halted the masquerade and had never, she said, told fortunes again. Now Millicent was to return to Ireland.

On our final walk over Mendip, I mentioned diffidently that I had started a novel and would she like to hear a page or two? So, in our sunny cottage at Shipham, I began to read the seventeen hand-written foolscap pages. Suddenly she sat up and exclaimed, "This is *good*!" and so opened a door into long hours of hard work and happiness. Soon chapters were flying to and fro across the Irish Sea for discussion and criticism. That novel did not reach publication — but the next one did.

In those early farmhouse days the discovery of *The Timeless Moment*, by Warner Allen, led to the breathtaking fascination with Time as we know it and the "Eternal Now" of God.

Reading then included Dunne's *The Serial Universe* and *An Adventure*, by Miss Moberly and Miss Jourdain, the two ladies who walked back into the time of Marie Antoinette, whom they saw in the gardens of the Trianon when the messenger came to warn her of the approaching mob, an incident authenticated by history.

Years later I discovered *Time and Man* by J. B. Priestley. This tome, unfortunately now out of print, has been trundled to and fro between library and farmhouse on numerous occasions until, being relegated to the reference department, it can no longer be borrowed. In this book, J. B. Priestley sets out his theory of the three Times: Time One as experienced now, second by second: Time Two, of the imagination when the mind moves freely between past and future and Time Three, in which he suggests that after death, misunderstandings between two persons in Time One can be "re-played" so to speak and resolved. I hope he is right.

A phrase from Clare Cameron's poem, "Between the Farmhouse and the Wood," recalls vividly one autumn day when I was standing by the gate at the end of the farmyard leading into Longwood. The perfection of orange, gold and tawny brown as the sun filtered through the beech leaves beneath a deep blue sky, invoked a feeling of infinite sadness at the inevitable passing of such glory and the longing to grasp and hold the beauty of the scene. Then came *my* Timeless Moment. I knew in a flash that nothing, literally nothing, could take this moment from me. It was part of the total experience which makes up the essential "me" for time and for eternity or, as I think it is better expressed, the Eternal Now. This I believe to be profoundly true.

Meanwhile daily time flies and there are still so many books to be read. My great hope is that, if the body should become old and worn out, eyesight and a clear brain may be retained to allow one to read. It is sad that a book loved and devoured in the reading, yet becomes hazy in the memory and difficult to recall. Somewhere in his writings — in *Miracles*, I believe — C. S. Lewis had the marvellous idea that, when we pass through the gate of death, all the books which one has enjoyed will remain vivid there. I have been laughed at for this idea of heaven as a vast library, but could there not be a grain of truth in it, however crudely expressed? The treasures of great minds, descriptions of places one will never see, the exploration into realms of philosophy and science — all become woven into the essential personality to be carried into future life. I hope it may be so.

Before the war I had learnt to ride at a riding school in Epping Forest, urged on by my mother who thought that the exercise and fresh air after bouts of bronchitis would be beneficial. This had involved a long bus journey and road work before reaching the forest rides. On the farm it was different. Christopher was easily caught and brought in from the field and the whole expanse of Mendip lay at our doorstep, and with Tom at my side we revelled in the gallops across a forty-acre field called the Goss, or across Blackdown. Sometimes Tom's brother joined us. As he urged his horse on with a "sss---ssss---sss", Christopher's ears went back; he showed the whites of his eyes and I concentrated on merely staying on his back. It was wildly exhilarating for Christopher liked to stay in front. If by chance he fell behind other horses, he was apt to turn sharply at right angles and gallop on to the peril of his rider who was likely to continue in a forward direction unless continually on the alert.

Tom rode him to hounds sometimes and then Christopher resembled a rocking horse, bucking and rearing in eagerness to set off. Tom said he was a natural jumper, easily clearing the stone walls of Mendip. But I was always thankful to see horse and rider safely home. Such preparations there were for a day's hunting! Harness and boots must shine, clothes be brushed and stock starched, sandwich cases and flasks filled, while the horses were brushed and curry-combed, tails washed and plaited, till the animals shone like silk.

In the early days Tom, his brother and the German prisoner-of-war who acted as Tom's groom, had to hack miles to the Meet and worse still, miles home afterwards. But still the horses must be rubbed down, fed and watered before the weary riders came in to eat and fall asleep. Saturday evenings were not very convivial, but I had my books and knitting and was happy in an armchair by the fire. Later, the brothers bought a horse-box which took the drudgery from attending a Meet. To this day Tom embroiders a car ride over Mendip with memories of walls jumped, hedges cleared and fields across which they galloped. While I disapprove of hunting, one can understand the exhilaration of the chase to men brought up to horses from their earliest days. I always asked, "Did you have a good day?" never "Did you kill?" In fact, I do not think they very often did.

During the war years village and social life flourished, despite the fact that a visit to friends was a major undertaking, after first having hoarded sufficient petrol coupons for the journey.

One day, Millicent and her husband walked the five miles from Priddy to suggest my taking the part of Lady Catherine de Bourgh in an excerpt from Jane Austen's *Pride and Prejudice*. "Of *course* you can," urged Tom when I demurred, and that was the start of many productions in Priddy village school by the light of oil lamps. Millicent has a gift for producing plays, welding together a most unlikely group of people, many without any acting experience, into a cohesive team. The blacked-out hall filled to capacity for performances of *The Bishop's Candlesticks* from Victor Hugo's *Les Misérables*, and another successful effort was a play about Robespierre and the French Revolution — ambitious topics for a village group. It was great fun coping with inadequate facilities, to put it mildly. Somehow the men built a portable stage from planks; costumes were manufactured from bits and pieces and ladies boiled water on primus stoves to provide the welcome cups of tea to which each member of the cast contributed a little from their ration. Milk was no problem as we had farmers and their wives involved, but the rule was, "Bring your own sugar". Owing to petrol rationing, rehearsals were often held in the vicarage after Evensong. Church attendance boomed!

I wonder how I, coming from a sheltered London background, never let out alone at night, undertook such journeys without hesitation, in second-hand cars liable to break down, across miles of wild Mendip country armed only with a pepper pot against possible molestation. I never had to use it.

One wet, windy evening after a group of us had spent the evening at Millicent's home we reluctantly put on macs, rain hats and wellingtons. My car would not start, of course. My succession of small, secondhand cars never did start well. Long after the rest of the party had departed down the drive and Millicent had shut the door against the storm, I was struggling with the long starting handle to coax a spark of life into the mass of inert metal. Nothing in the mechanical world is so dead as a car that will not start. When I had almost given up hope it chugged noisily to life and I departed thankfully for my five-mile drive across the inky blackness of Mendip. That is no exaggeration: in those wartime days we drove with black paper gummed over our side lights and only a hole the size of an old halfpenny in the centre, and on that stormy night there was not a star visible. The occasional farmhouse or cottage by the roadside showed no glimmer of light through the black-out. I was alone in a world of driving rain which swept, unhindered by the stone walls, across the landscape. The way seemed endless at night, as my eyes strained to steer clear of the muddy verges. Narrow roads leading to field or farmhouse branched off occasionally, making it difficult to decide in the blackness exactly where one was.

Then, splashing through water lying in the hollow at the foot of a hill, the engine spluttered and stopped. Sheer panic set my pulse racing. Terrified that the stranded car might cause an accident — suppose an army vehicle should come along? — I tied a failing torch to the bumper, defying the blackout, and began the long walk back to Millicent's house to beg a night on her settee.

At first light I was trudging back to the car. A friendly tractor driver happened to pass that way. He grinned, attached a chain and towed the Baby Austin, known familiarly as "the Matchbox", until the engine came sluggishly to life. I reached home before anyone was up and slipped into bed beside Tom, my husband, who had drugged a heavy cold with whisky the previous evening and was still asleep. It was months before he was told of that exploit.

Our farmhouse stood at the head of a wooded valley leading to Cheddar Gorge and the nearest farm was over a mile away. There was, of course, no bus service: our link with the outside world was the telephone. Looking back, I wonder how it was that a timid Londoner should have ventured to drive in thick fog across Mendip, but alternate Fridays were Old Time Dance nights and one risked any difficulty to get to Priddy. Millicent and I danced our way through waltzes, tangoes, veletas and the stately cotillion and were whirled around in the Lancers in the company of young and old who gathered for an evening's enjoyment in those grim days. In the school room, with blacked-out windows, warmed by a round, black, iron stove on top of which stood a big, black kettle, hung two oil lamps and a gramophone supplied the music. At half time spoonfuls of tea and sugar were pooled from our rations to make a hot, strong brew with the occasional luxury of a biscuit. Then, on with the dance with the hazard of the return journey looming nearer. There must have been bright, starlit nights, but the dark, foggy ones blot out their memory.

Those were anxious days, especially when we were expecting invasion. All sign posts were taken down and only local inhabitants were allowed along roads lined with tanks and army vehicles, on production of a pass. The issue of vouchers worth ten shillings (50p) per person with which to obtain food from a secret store, in case of emergency, underlined the seriousness of the situation.

Our farm was requisitioned as an R.A.F. centre and we were obliged to lodge and board a number of "Rafs". Five hundred yards away, on the summit of Blackdown, a decoy was set up, the object of which was to trick the enemy bombers into thinking that the area was Bristol once their planes had dropped flares on that city. Not a very healthy situation for us! After the war, workmen arrived to remove our Anderson shelters and were horrified to learn that we had not even been offered one.

There was one scare when an enemy sea-plane was being chased very low over the house. There was a tremendous bang. As the 'phone shrilled, part of it flew across the room. That was the "red" warning for the decoy to be lit. Unfortunately the Sergeant and his men were off duty and by the time they were located and had raced back, the decoy was lit three quarters of an hour after the mine had dropped.

Next morning there was a huge hole on Blackdown which subsequently filled with rain-water and made an excellent pond for cattle. There were other "perks" too. Scattered around were yellow nylon parachutes, so that most of my friends received birthday and Christmas presents of coupon-free petticoats. First one had to unpick yards and yards of seams, carefully winding the yellow thread for future use, and then we spread the sections of parachute on the floor to pin on the pattern to the best advantage. This was our first experience of nylon.

The nylon cords attached to the parachutes had their uses too. When leather reins were broken and replacements or repairs unobtainable, our horses had elegant double-plaited nylon reins. It was the German prisoners who plaited those reins, when they were billeted on us for farm work during the latter days of the war after the R.A.F. had left.

We had Italians too, all living harmoniously together. Arriving home from school — for I was still teaching — I allowed myself fifteen minutes relaxation and then the first job was to cut mounds of bread and margarine and to contrive something for tea from the rations for our mixed family. Then the next day's dinner had to be prepared for one of the men to cook. Tom took charge of breakfasts and became adept at making dried egg omelette flavoured with herbs. During the evenings we sat round the kitchen table with notebooks and pencils, and learnt something of each other's languages.

One of the Germans used to accompany me when I rode Christopher, a horse given as a wedding present since his owner could no longer obtain fodder for him. Tom could not always spare the time and did not care for me to venture far alone. The prisoners were a splendid lot, completely trustworthy and helpful. One Italian, who was a tailor, helped me to make a dress. Another remained in the neighbourhood after the war as a true and loyal friend.

We knew, of course, about the major events of the war, remote though it was from Mendip. One day in June 1940, S.B.G., Rover and I spent the day at Burnham. It was warm and sunny and the sea looked like watered silk as we walked along the sands, pausing at times to gaze at the perfection of sea and sky. We ate our sandwiches sitting among the sand dunes, leaning against the coarse grass. But S.B.G. was restless. "There's something going on," she said. "I don't know what, something to do with little boats". Once or twice before, S.B.G. had seemed to sense things unknown to ourselves, so Rover and I became restless and disturbed too.

How we returned from Burnham I do not remember — but when we reached Cheddar the news had broken about the little boats plying to and fro across the Channel to rescue our soldiers from Dunkirk.

They were grim days which followed. Impressions are all muddled: The Battle of Britain; the loss of submarines which imperilled our food supply; the loss of the *Prince of Wales* and the *Repulse*; the raid on Pearl Harbour and, always, the very real threat of invasion. I was sitting in the dark at my Grandmother's, by the glow of a small fire, when Churchill's voice warned us that he could offer, "nothing but blood, sweat, toil and tears", saying that we would fight on the beaches, and fight in the streets. It was at Grandmother's too, that we heard King George VI's moving speech. Forced into kingship which he neither expected nor desired, in that first broadcast to the nation on radio at Christmas, overcoming with tremendous courage the impediment in his speech, he endeared himself to us all. Later, by his sharing with the Queen the sorrows of his people in the bomb-blasted streets and his refusal to send his children to the comparative security of America, he inspired devotion in us ordinary folk.

On June 6th, 1944, my mother's birthday, the Mulberry Harbour was towed across the Channel. We heard of this marvel but could not imagine how such a thing could be possible. Gradually news of our troops' advance with the Americans, and the crumbling of the enemy, filtered through and we knew that the end was at hand. On V.E. day we celebrated the end of the war in Europe with Millicent and her husband as church bells, hushed for so long, only to be used in case of invasion, rang joyfully throughout the land and there were street parties in town and village.

Daily life went on much as usual, though it was a relief no longer to be obliged to carry gas masks or for children to dive beneath their desks when the siren sounded. That had seemed fun to them at first but when the warning had sounded near the end of school time it meant that weary teachers must keep hungry, disgruntled children till the "All Clear" set them free. That had not been fun.

Rationing of food, clothing and petrol continued for several years. The prisoners went home, apart from one Italian who has become a faithful friend.

It seemed that as an evacuated teacher I would be out of a job until, one day, J.J., the local headmaster who had welcomed us on arrival, called me to his room and asked, since one of his staff was retiring, would I like to apply for the job? I did so, delighted that it was an infants' vacancy and remained in the school until retirement thirty-two years after evacuation.

CHAPTER SEVEN

Farming Tapestry

THE FARMHOUSE was limestone-built, south facing with mullioned windows. It was a lovely house at least 400 years old. We had the smaller part: a large kitchen-cum-living room, and a large sunny dining-room with wide cushioned window seat overlooking the walled garden and, beyond that, Longwood. A closed staircase led to the two large bedrooms and a little one. With our own entrance we were technically separate, despite a communicating door into the part in which Tom's mother lived with others of her family.

Settling in to the new life was not easy. Regarded as an interloper — as indeed I was — Tom's mother did not welcome me.

Tom, who had interrupted his career as a male nurse to come home to help his father during a difficult period, felt trapped when, after the latter's death and the outbreak of war, he was obliged to remain on the farm in the interest of food production. What he really wanted to do was to get back to nursing. It was a long time before he could return to his chosen career, but meanwhile he continued his service with St John Ambulance Brigade rendering valuable service when bombs fell on Bristol and in villages nearer home. Local farm workers often came to him too, with cuts and bruises for first aid.

During those first weeks there were innumerable pinpricks to make me feel small, if I should dare to deal with the travelling grocer before my mother-in-law and when I took potatoes from a full sack when older ones remained in another, I felt as shrivelled as the potatoes themselves at the tirade which followed! At least I was away at school all day. Weekends were difficult at first, but a compromise was gradually reached. On Saturday evenings, Tom took his mother to the "local" while I stayed at home. Few were the books to which I still had access and, if the battery for the wireless happened to run out, there was nothing to hear but the occasional screech of an owl or the bark of a fox. Staying at home was probably a subconscious bid to state my own individuality in the face of those who did not like me, lonely though it was.

But Sundays were the reverse. Having left me at home on Saturday, Tom rushed to get the milking done in time to take me to church on Sunday evening. His brother, who did not care what time he finished work, was never in a hurry to get out after dinner. But Tom usually managed it, scrambling into the suit I had laid out ready and saucering a cup of tea. I was on tenterhooks as the minutes ticked by for, apart from the actual service, this was a gesture, something we did together despite great odds.

The church, where Millicent's husband was vicar, lay five miles away across Mendip in the village of Priddy. The present building, dating from 1352, was dimly lit by oil-lamps lovingly cared for by Bertie W., well over seventy by then, who was warden, sidesman, bell-ringer and sexton rolled into one. He led the congregation in the singing at his chosen pace, no matter if it were quicker or slower than that set by the organist. Bertie had already dug his own grave and requested that at his death mourners should wear a rose instead of bringing wreaths. Fortunately he died in summer so we could all wear a rose as he wished. His funeral was the first at which I heard an Easter hymn, sung at his request. It was a joyful occasion.

Round the walls of the church are the original stone seats for the use of the elderly and infirm in the days before other seating was provided. Hanging in a glass case opposite the door there is still an altar frontal of early English embroidery on Italian damask, which was retrieved by Millicent from the vicarage garret where it had been rolled into a bundle. Restored by the Guild of Church Needlewomen the hanging was memorable. The well-loved vicar told us from the pulpit that it was "half a thousand years old" (which seemed much longer than a mere 500 years!) He was a poet and through his eyes we saw worshippers down the centuries, generation after generation, kneeling at the rail before the altar frontal.

After the service we went to the cosy, grey stone cottage where Tom's sister Ada lived. Beside a blazing fire, Ada managed to give us tea, sandwiches and sometimes a homemade slice of cake in spite of the rationing. She was so kind: the only person in Tom's family who made me feel at home and wanted. Ada had not much money but she was always giving. To stretch her husband's modest wages, she took young men learning forestry or girls working for local farmers, and welcomed holiday visitors, into her little home without modern conveniences, making friendships which have lasted till the present, when Ada is in her eighties.

Ada has a gift for saying "the wrong thing" in all innocence. I remember, when she was describing a certain visitor from Wells Cathedral, she added, "*I* get on all right with her — although she's stuck-up and stand-offish just like you!" One could not take offence; all the more credit to her for her welcome to her home if that is the impression I gave!

Being extremely shy I found it difficult to be at ease until knowing people very well. Tom is the opposite, making friends easily. He was proud of me and in order not to let him down, I took on jobs such as vice-president of the W.I. and gave talks to Mothers' Union on education and local history, which formerly would have seemed impossible. I opened doors for him too, introducing him to books and ballet and to holidays abroad, so it has been a two-way relationship. Differences of opinion and clash of personality arise of course. Tom is quick-tempered, but I refuse to "blow up", fearing to say too much, so usually keep quiet and walk away, probably a maddening attitude to the person concerned.

I was still teaching, having by now been absorbed into the local school. Each morning I waited, books under arm, for Tom to rush in from the cowshed and take me the six miles down to school. It was an old car and on one occasion when it broke down I decided to ride a horse, old Greybird, leaving her in a friendly farmer's field. For the first day all went well: she trotted amiably downhill and returned at a sober uphill pace. The next day I was persuaded to take Pixie, a younger and more lively mare. But Pixie hated pigs and as we neared the pig farm halfway down to Cheddar she stopped, snorted and began to prance around. She bucked, she reared, turning in tight circles. Somehow I stuck on her back, but nothing would persuade Pixie to pass those pigs. So we headed back for home. She trotted smartly uphill and we cantered along the grass verges, which I would normally have enjoyed but for the thought of the grins as heads poked out of the cowhouses at the clip-clop of her hooves down the yard. So much for my independence: I was taken, ignominiously as it seemed, on the back of my brother-in-law's motorcycle down to school.

Coming home I would start to walk wearily up the steep hill with a case full of books to mark, hoping every moment to see Tom appearing in the distance. So many things can happen to delay a farmer; I did not blame him but it was hard going, especially in the rain.

Then one day he stopped the car, got out and said, "Move over. You can drive home." So I learnt to drive. It was a nerve-wracking business for both of us. Tom was scared and that made me worse. There were no schools of motoring during the war; no driving tests. One simply learnt to drive by driving. One evening, Tom actually pulled the handbrake out in his anxiety to stop the car when I was heading for a gatepost. It was almost impossible to get spare parts for civilian cars so we just did without a handbrake. Then came the day when he sent me off to school alone. The battery was not too good so the car had to be started on the handle, an iron bar which one turned, at the risk of kickback resulting in a broken arm, till the engine roared into life. I could not manage this so I was instructed to drive without stopping to a garage in Cheddar Gorge, leave the car and walk to school and back in the afternoon when Mr Maine would start it up for me.

I realised afterwards that I was sent off like this on the day my mother was arriving from London at Cheddar station, to "show how clever I was!" I had to leave the car running while meeting her and we started off home. *Of course*, I stalled the engine half-way up Hundred Acres Batch, the steepest hill. What to do? I couldn't get out of gear to try to start on the handle without a handbrake. Deadlock. Then mother decided to walk back the half mile to the last farm we had passed in search of help and arrived back with the farmer before any other vehicle had passed me. The farmer put stones from the wall behind the wheels, started on the handle and obligingly drove up the top of the hill while mother and I puffed up behind. That hill remained a nightmare, especially when it was deeply rutted with frozen snow. Never had I even imagined such an experience in the sheltered London years!

Later I acquired a high "matchbox" Austin Seven for £54 and sold it later for £44. At least it had all its parts. Similar cars can occasionally be seen in museums now! In those days, the R.A.F. were building cairns on Blackdown to deter enemy planes from landing and every day a huge coachload of airmen would meet me as I trundled slowly uphill, and would wave cheerfully. One day however, we met at the narrowest part of the road with a ditch on either side. I stopped, facing the grey monster, too terrified to try to reverse between those ditches with all those grinning faces watching. I just got out and waved to them till one friendly airman hopped out and reversed for me.

In 1947, that worst of winters, cars stood in garages for three whole months on Mendip. Snow obliterated hedge and road alike in unbroken whiteness. The idea of ringing up and saying that I could not get down to school just did not occur to me; I walked down the six miles each Monday, wrapped in an old hunting mac of Tom's over a thick coat with balaclava and wellingtons. On sunny days the walk was a joy with snow sparkling all around, twigs encased finger-thick in ice which tinkled as they touched in the slight breeze. There were cornices of snow carved by the wind. The delicacy of those knife-edges was a source of continual wonder beneath a cloudless blue sky.

There was one morning when the road between Tynings Farm and the top of Hundred Acres Batch was a series of cornices four or five feet high, surmounting perfectly hollowed drifts where the wind had whipped through the wire fence. As I negotiated the rise and fall of the lovely drifts, spoiling their perfect symmetry, a small figure approached. It was our Italian plodding up to work. When we met, we solemnly shook hands, a symbolic gesture, and continued on our opposite ways, using each other's tracks.

On Friday evenings I used to manage to get to Shipham, halfway up Mendip, to meet Tom there. He had walked down

Charterhouse in the Winter of 1947

so far to buy groceries for the family — his uncle and aunt had been evacuated to the other part of the house — to swell the numbers there.

Before starting on our long walk up to the farm there was always a hot meal ready for us, prepared by a kindly neighbour, still one of our best friends. The delicious scent of roasting beef still transports me to the warmth and comfort of that cottage surrounded by the ice and snow of 1947.

Nowadays the roads are kept passable by snow ploughs, so the passage of milk lorries is more or less possible with care in even the worst weather, but in 1947 the milk was not collected for weeks. Tom and his brother filled every available churn, a disused bath was scrubbed out, every container from house and dairy filled with milk till there was not an empty vessel in the place. The thaw came suddenly: milk was collected and, thanks to having been frozen, not a drop was lost.

I am proud that in the log-book of Cheddar Primary school it is recorded that throughout the severe winters of 1947 and 1963 I never missed a day's school through bad weather. The school did not close — of course! The headmaster, J.J., as everyone called him, was tough and expected his children and staff to be tough too. Though the lavatories were frozen and had to be thawed by kettles of boiling water brought from the schoolhouse, though there was no heating and no school dinners, we wrapped up in thick clothes and just carried on. From time to time, classes could be heard jumping around in the classrooms, and at playtimes. J.J. organised slides in the playground. Attendance kept up well.

J.J. himself was a remarkable character. Headmaster since the age of twenty-nine, "my school" was the core of his life. Self-centred, and boring to outsiders once he started on his favourite topic, he was a strong influence in the village in his early days, organising outings, sports and social events at a time when there was no entertainment laid on at the press of a button. He knew and remembered every child who had passed through his hands until retirement. After that traumatic event, seeing him approach in the village, one knew one would be buttonholed for at least half an hour to hear of past pupils who had written to, or visited him, racking one's brains the while to recall the names and faces of so many years ago. He was a good headmaster, and I have cause to be grateful to him.

The climax of that frozen winter of 1947 came one weekend. The milking cows were kept in houses, being let out to the slippery yard to drink at tanks when the ice had been broken, but the young cattle were housed half a mile away in Longhouse, the centre portion of which was stocked with hay. Every morning Tom and his brother had to go out to feed and water those heifers.

This particular Saturday, they found that a two-year-old had calved prematurely and though the calf was dead the mother was alive. But how to get her home? No tractor could get there. Finally they took off a field gate and came home for Blossom, the cart-horse. She struggled back with the heifer on the improvised sledge with the men pushing and pulling. Miraculously, she lived. But when Tom came indoors, his discarded mac stood by itself on the kitchen floor. Such was life on a Mendip farm that year. I shall not forget the night when I was warm and safe in the house of a kind friend at Cheddar, hearing Tom say on the 'phone, "I just don't want to wake up in the morning to face another day" — and there was nothing I could do to help.

It was during that winter, on an unexpected day's holiday, I decided to surprise Tom by walking home to the farm from our cottage in Shipham, which we had bought in the latter days of the war. It was a sunny morning with little snow lying in the village. I set off gaily, expecting an invigorating walk. Up Holloway was easy, then down into Water Valley. Here the snow was lying thickly and I soon discovered that there was ice beneath. But I crossed the frozen stream and climbed to the far side of the valley crowned by forestry pines and firs. Suddenly the sky darkened, the wind rose, snow fell and in a few minutes I could scarcely see the path. Desperately I tried to keep my footing. What if I fell and twisted an ankle? No one knew where I was. Struggling on, the snow was driven into my face till all I could see were points of red and green. Nearing exhaustion I cleared the valley and knew that half a mile along the track was a farmhouse. The farmer's wife was amazed to see me emerging from the blizzard. I shall not forget the warmth of that kitchen or the mug of hot, sweet cocoa thrust into my hands. The farmer came in for a hot drink and soon I was on the back of his tractor clinging to him as we jolted over the frozen ruts. Tom realized what might have happened and hid his concern by berating me for being so foolish as to attempt the walk without even telling anybody where I was going.

From the beginning I tried to help on the farm, but it was all so new after suburban London life. Rigged up in white milking coat and cap, I sat nervously on a three-legged stood under Daisy, a "quiet" cow and tried to achieve a stream of milk like those which issued into the pails of the other milkers. My wrists soon ached with the squeezing action but little else happened. Daisy knew that something strange was afoot and would not let down her milk. Then Tom or one of the men would start her off and I managed to fill half a pail but could not strip her completely. Daisy became restive, the movement of her soft, heavy body nearly upsetting my balance as I sat with the bucket clasped between my knees. When the milking was done, there were the pails to wash and put in the sterilizer. I got on better with this, leaving Tom to help clean the stalls when the cows had been turned into a field some distance up the road.

I enjoyed cleaning out the calves, too. It was hard work, but the sight of contented animals on a bed of fresh straw was reward enough. Once milking started they mooed till Tom arrived with buckets of milk, sucked in the early days "through" his finger. When warm, sunny days arrived they were turned out, bucking and leaping about in their new-found freedom, among them a calf of my own, a gentle Guernsey named Noëlle — a Christmas present from Tom.

We had hens too. The orchard of old cider apple trees was considered Tom's, to do with as he liked, and here we had several hen houses lined with nests which could be opened from outside. They were "run around" hens, of course. As the henhouse doors were opened each morning they clucked their pleasure and it was surprising how their voices varied as they jostled each other down the wooden ramps, pecking eagerly at the scattered corn. Occasionally, Tom would set a broody hen and I watched daily for the first hatching, a never-ending miracle to a town-bred girl. No sooner were the chickens out of the shell than they began pecking around, running after their mother as she clucked around the farmyard calling to them as she scratched and scattered grains.

In the evening the hens must be shut in and a thorough search made along the hedges to find any loiterers. It was important to do this at the right moment of dusk: left out too long some flew into the trees to roost and would not come down. It was a joy to collect the baskets full of eggs from the straw-filled nests and to know that all was safe for the night.

But there were tragedies too. Even in daytime a fox could work havoc, leaving a mass of feathers in places but, worse still, a trail of dead hens. Those were bitter days. During one summer holiday I took my books and knitting up to the orchard and sat there, allowing our "brown girls" some hours of freedom, feeling rather like the Frenchwomen we had seen among the Cevennes, knitting all day as they watched their goats.

One of Tom's hunters, Lassie, lived in the orchard one spring, for she was in foal for the first time. As her time drew near we were continually popping up to have a look at her. One Sunday morning we returned to the house for a cup of coffee. Some walkers passed the garden gate. "Fine foal you've got up there," commented one. We raced up and there was a beautiful filly with a white flash, already on her slender legs nuzzling her mother. Desirée, we named her, the longed-for foal.

Before long, she came at our call, teased us by taking the henhouse keys from the doors, so that we had to search for them in the grass and once she took a mouthful of my hair as I bent to retrieve them. At a month old, Tom decided she must learn to be led. A tiny halter was put on and together we attempted to lead her. With wide-spread legs the little creature defied the strength of the two of us pulling the rope. Suddenly she took a step and we collapsed backwards. Thereafter she followed wherever we led and when the time came for breaking in, Tom had no trouble at all, I simply held the bridle while Tom mounted. After one small buck she accepted him on her back. Lassie had many more foals but Desirée was our pride and joy.

We also had some calves who came running up to us as we went to the hens. Hay bales had to be carried up for them and buckets of water to replenish the trough, for unlike the fields, the orchard had no supply of running water. "Boy", a big black yearling, was very good at getting out — however good the hedge. On my way home from school it was not unusual to find him grazing by the roadside. Then there was nothing for it but to leave the car and try to get him back without bothering Tom.

When Tom was ill with pleurisy, the farm work was done by the men, but I looked after our hens and calves. It was hard work after a day at school, and mornings were hectic too. One day almost at Cheddar, I remembered the hens had not been let out, so back up the hill I went. I never forgot again.

In the early days I helped to put up barbed wire and we made scarecrows for the barley. It all helped to integrate me into the new life, and Tom and I got to know each other better. On the way home he would sometimes "lose" me; I'd be wandering along by the limestone walls, turning over stones to look for fossils, an interest developed after a lecture on geology. A borrowed *Introduction to Geology* led to many more books on the subject and later to lectures in Wells about Mendip and palaeontology, and lately to the Open University. Tom became interested too. One day he brought in a honeycomb coral found in the orchard, a relic of the days when Mendip lay beneath a warm sea. Together we found ammonites and belemnites at Lyme Regis and Bridgwater Bay. One of my happiest snaps is of Tom lifting from a rock pool on the coast of Sligo, a foot-long coral loosened by wave action from the rocks where they lie in masses. We always visit our "secret" beach when visiting Sligo — there is never anyone else there. Pebble polishing too, is a fascinating hobby giving an excuse to bring home pebbles and stones gathered on holiday.

Towards the end of our farming days one of the men decided to change his job for that of driving a milk lorry, leaving Tom and the cowman to do all the early morning work. All went well during the first weeks, but as the mornings became darker everything went wrong. The cowman hurt his back and was off sick; the electricity failed for some unknown reason. Poor Tom was alone in a cold dark world each morning and I made up my mind to help him. Oil lamps have never been my strong point but I went to the sheds to light the lanterns and hang them on the walls while Tom fetched the cows. Frankly, I was terrified that I would turn the wick down instead of up or do something incredibly stupid to those ancient lamps. I have never felt so miserably inefficient as when struggling with them.

The second day will stick in my memory for ever. It was a morning of such ferocity of wind and rain that even Tom had not experienced. Wrapped from head to foot in coats, scarves, woolly hats, macs and wellingtons we went out into the blackness after a scalding cup of tea. With shaking fingers I tried to light those lanterns but the gale whistled through every crack in the cowhouse doors, blowing out the flame however I tried to shield it. Then I realised that Lassie, our cow dog, was beside me instead of following Tom. How would he manage without the dog? There was only one thing to do. "Come, Lassie," I said, "we must help to get the cows."

Fortunately I knew in which direction Tom had gone and

stumbled after him up Colliers Lane. Here, sheltered a little by high banks and tall trees, my shouts reached him and he waited for us to catch up. "I'll stay and help you," I panted, fishing in my mac pockets for a small torch. "You'll need that in this blackness," said Tom grimly.

Once in the field the full force of the gale tore at us and the rain beat mercilessly down. How would we find the cows in this darkness? Tom shouted in my ear to take one side of the field — but to keep away from the trees. "Branches blowing down," he bawled. Away he and Lassie went and I was alone in the black, raging wilderness and I remember thinking in a detached way, "If Joan could see me now!"

Stumbling around, the time seemed endless as we searched ten acres and fifteen acres. At last, utterly defeated, scarcely able to stand, our torches wavered towards each other. "Go home," shouted Tom. "I'll cut across Pond Close and four acres. The wretched creatures may have crashed the hedge."

He found them, thirty-six in all, clustered by a hedge. Some stupid person had left connecting gates open. The milk was barely ready for the lorry that morning and the cows lay in the stalls that night.

There were good times too: winter evenings by a roaring log fire, surrounded, to Tom's amusement, by a variety of books, knitting, sewing, notepaper — everything one might need for an evening's enjoyment. Tom began rug making. Later he made two complete carpets for our Mendip cottage.

There were spring days when the dawn chorus filled the world with the glory of birdsong. Then the woods and lanes were starred with primroses and "woods and brakes washed wet like lakes" with bluebells. "I hope," I remember saying to Millicent, "that I shall never get *used* to spring!" I never did.

It was during those early years that Millicent and I gathered masses of primroses in Ebbor Gorge one Good Friday and wrote with them, on a bed of moss, "He is Risen" to decorate for Easter Day the ancient church in Priddy, that lonely Mendip village.

CHAPTER EIGHT

Changes in Farming

DURING my many years on the farm I witnessed, without realising it, a complete revolution, from the days of horse-drawn implements and manual labour to mechanisation: from thatched haystacks to the bales packed neatly into Dutch barns.

The first summer of our marriage was one of continual blue days — or so it seems, looking back over the years. Incredibly far-off seems that time now when, after a day's teaching in the school in the valley, I would trudge out to the hayfield with a basketful of sandwiches and cake, flasks of tea and bottled lemonade. Men flung themselves down in the shade of the hedge for a brief respite, speaking little, content to eat and drink and savour the relaxation. Then back to work.

Anxious to be of use, I took a pique, a long handled two-pronged fork with which to lift loose hay. This was difficult for a beginner; most of the hay dropped off, so my effort did not help much.

A base of bracken, cut by scythe on Blackdown and carried to the field by horse and waggon, had been laid down and on this the rick rose rapidly as the rick maker spread the hay, which was tossed up equally over the area. This was a skilled job, for a badly made rick could collapse into a heap and be ruined by rain.

At the beginning of the war the horse-drawn hay collector was replaced by a Fordson tractor with a wooden hay sweep in front, which was in use for the first time that summer. The pitchers were kept very busy as even that modest little tractor brought in loads much faster than had been possible by the horse-drawn method. Small though it was compared with the many-geared, multiple horse-powered monsters of today equipped with cab and ear muffs for the driver, it marked the

*Scything Corn, which Tom
can just remember*

first step towards mechanisation. Tom was proud of his tractor and used to tell me how, when he was a boy, the hay had been piled into small cocks and then tossed on to a horse-drawn waggon to be hauled to the rick.

As the rick rose to shoulder height, a ladder was placed against the side so that piquefuls of hay were lifted to a man on the ladder who raised it to the rick-maker. Finally the stack was roofed and combed with a wooden hay rake to ensure that the rain would run off rather than soak in. Later, the ricks were thatched with straw from the harvest field. Each field had one or more ricks according to its crop and acreage, to be cut out with a hay knife for winter feeding. Haymaking was a continuous process, given good weather. While one field was being "made" the next was being cut with horse-drawn mowing machine.

In the delicious scent of the cool of the evening I was filled with a great contentment. The hayfield with its distant gleam of the sea seemed so completely cut off from the world of gas masks, of queueing for rations and the constant nagging anxiety that this "phoney war" must end in unimaginable horror. But there was a feeling of guilt sometimes that I was enjoying an idyllic summer while, for those left at home in London, life was a grey monotony.

I was soon to experience the reverse side of the coin concerning farm life. There were summers when constant rain prevented Tom from even mowing the grass. But the worst weather was the time of alternate rain and sunshine. Once cut, the grass was left a day or so to dry, then turned by the swathe turner drawn by a horse, while the swathes round the edges of the field were tossed by a man with a pique — or sometimes by me.

After drying for a couple of days, the tedder was brought out and harnessed to Damsel or Blossom and the field was lined with long rollers of hay ready for the hay sweep. Tom and the men would spend the whole day and come home tired, but jubilant, saying, "We'll get that field tomorrow." But if the following day came in wet the gloom was well-nigh unbearable. All that time, money for wages and diesel oil wasted, but worst of all the hay might rot with the damp. At best, the work must be done again: the hay spread out and the whole process repeated. During such changeable weather in "double summer time" they would work till 10 o'clock, snatch a cup of tea, too tired to eat, and start the milking. I used to stagger out about 11 p.m. and begin to wash the milk tins, thinking sometimes of Joan and Carrie snugly asleep. With the advent of the prisoners-of-war the situation eased; then a couple of men could be sent home from the field earlier to cope with the milking.

As new inventions appeared, life was a little less arduous. We considered ourselves modernised by the purchase of an elevator which took the labour out of pitching, but still the turning, rollering and sweeping must be done with tractor and horses and much toil.

Years later came the baler, that great shiny machine which binds the cut grass, leaving bales dotted over the field. Then all hands were called out to stand the bales on end in groups to allow the free passage of air. Then came the tractor and trailer and the back-breaking job of lifting bales on to the trailer and off again to be stacked in the barn, an interminable job. I could not lift the bales but sometimes drove the tractor, a tricky job to keep it just at walking pace for the men to load. With a man on the trailer stacking the bales it was imperative to drive smoothly for fear of dislodging him. At the end of such a session, my whole body quivered with the strain and the motion of the engine.

The next mechanical aid was a Stackhy — a kind of mobile elevator which lifted the baled hay on to the trailer, but they still had to be manhandled in the barn.

It was during wartime that the revolutionary idea of silage making arrived. The grass was cut, raised by suction and blown into a Weeks trailer and unloaded into a silage pit. Surprisingly, the cows enjoyed the evil smelling end product, and it certainly made less work and took some of the hazard of the weather out of farming.

It was in school holiday time during those early years on the farm that Tom came in one suffocatingly hot day. "We're frightfully rushed," he said, "working against time to get a field of hay. Could you come and rake a field, please?"

"I don't think I could manage. . . ." I began.

"Of course you can, dear," was the reply. "Put on a pair of my trousers and come out to fifteen acres."

With much trepidation I walked out to the field where Tom was harnessing Blossom to the horse rake. "Jump up," he said. "It's quite simple really. As you reach the swathe just pull this handle then release it, but keep the horse moving all the time. I'm off to make the rick in the next field."

So there was I, perched on an iron seat on a lovely sunny day. But there was no time to look at the view of the sparkling sea at Weston from my vantage point. "Go on, Blossom," I said. So far, so good. She ambled forwards, but when we reached the first roller, I lifted the handle with my left hand and jerked her to a halt with my right hand. This occurred at the next dozen or so rollers with Damsel looking reproachfully round now and again as I tried to disassociate the action of my left hand from that of my right. It was Blossom's good sense which won the day. Realising that she had a complete novice "in control" she calmly carried on regardless of my tugging at the reins. After a couple of hours I was relieved to see Tom approaching. "Well done," he said. "You've made a good job of that. We may get this field in now." I stayed to help and as we pitched the last load the first thunder spots fell. We were drenched before reaching the house, but inwardly glowing with the satisfaction of a field saved.

Another occasion on which I was called out to help was on Christmas Day. Having washed up and settled down to hear the King's speech, the peace was shattered by a request to "come and drive the tractor". So it was a case of off with my best dress and into a skirt and jersey, wellingtons, headscarf and gloves and out to the field. Tom put the tractor into first gear and, as he had to feed the cattle alone, it was my job to drive slowly round the snowy field full of icy ridges while he threw off the hay. It was bitterly cold and my hands were numb by the time we had finished.

Snow began to fall so we had to stay at home that evening instead of going to friends. Tom especially found it very quiet for he was used to having a houseful of visitors in his younger days. There was the wireless — but no television, and outside, nothing but snow for miles around.

In good years when the hay was gathered by mid-July, there was a period of general relaxation before harvest began and time to go to gymkhanas on Saturdays. With flasks and sandwiches we sat round the ring to catch up on local news and to discuss how the local riders had improved. We could not know on those far-off sunny afternoons that, ten years later, we would sit at home and watch those same youngsters on our television screens at Olympia, Badminton, Dublin or Hickstead.

During the war the Ministry of Agriculture decreed that each farm must grow a certain amount of cereals to help the war effort. Our quota was for oats, so gradually ploughed land took the place of pasture, and rough ground must be cleared, fertilised and seeded.

Corn ripens late on Mendip at 900 feet above sea level, so the weather was even more important to hill farmers than to those in the valley. In good years, greening ears turned to gold by early September. Then out came the binder. This machine with its revolving blades cut and bound the corn in sheaves.

Then came the job of stooking the sheaves to allow the air to pass through. In a twenty acre field, the sheaves seemed endless. Even wearing gloves, hands became rough and sore from the occasional thistles among the oats, ankles were pricked by the stubble and backs ached with the continual bend-lift-carry, till the field was dotted with stooks. Every available person was pressed into action: one year our two mothers came out to do their little bit. Tom's mother, then in her seventies, had been used to such work all her life and my mother placed the sheaves which I lifted.

Now, the stooks must stand for "three church bells", a worrying time in case the weather should break, in which case, even stooked corn could grow out. On the other hand, if it was ricked before the grain was dry, the result could be disaster by fermentation.

When dry the sheaves were piled on trailers and carried to the rickyard to be stacked. Next came the thatcher to roof the ricks.

When word went round that the thresher was coming, all other work, apart from milking, stopped and men gravitated to the Heath Robinson jumble of jolting machinery. Sheaves tossed on were shaken violently till the seed fell from the ears and was dribbled into a row of sacks at the end of the machine. Full sacks were removed, and replaced, necks tied and loaded on to the trailers to be stored in the barn. As the last sacks were carried home a sense of fulfillment settled over the farm; the crown of a year's hard work; the satisfaction of a job well done.

Towards the end of the war the combine harvester made its appearance; a near-miraculous machine, as it seemed at first, which cut, threshed and sacked the corn, throwing out the straw already bound into bundles, in a single operation. But it was not quite so simple as had first appeared. Gateways must be widened to admit the monster — *when* it was available. There was the delicate balance between the moment when the corn was ripe for cutting — not so ripe that the grain would fall from the ears — and the anxiety as to when the contractor would come, for so many farmers were waiting. The first year that we had forty acres in corn I looked anxiously each afternoon on the return from school, hoping the red dinosaur of a machine would be toiling up and down. It came at last — but only just in time.

There was one September evening the following year when Tom and I leant over the gate of that same field looking at the oats, tall, beautiful and golden. "The best we've ever had," he said softly. "The combine is leaving Small's first thing in the morning. It'll be here by nine. Just a couple of days' work instead of the weeks we used to put in." He passed his hand over his eyes. "What's the matter?" I asked. "Tired?"

"Oh it's nothing," was the reply, "just the head I get when a storm is brewing." A storm! I looked at him in alarm and in the same instant he realised the significance of his words. "It's hot and airless enough," I said. "Oh! it *couldn't*!"

"Hope not," he muttered, then turned away brusquely. "Come along. I have to be up extra early tomorrow to get the milk out."

We were awakened by the distant roll of thunder. Lying tense and helpless we heard the first heavy rain as the thunder increased in intensity and lightning split the sky. On and on it went but when at last it passed into reverberating rumbling the rain continued to beat mercilessly against the window panes. Neither spoke. There was nothing to say.

I had fallen into a restless sleep, but waking at first light found that Tom had already gone. I followed him to the gate at which we had leaned the previous evening. The barley was flattened in huge irregular patches.

"If the rain stops and the combine can get in, we may save some," he said, as I slipped my hand into his. But the rain continued intermittently for more than a week and the seed grew out.

Harvest Festival was difficult that year in the little church at Priddy. How could we joyfully sing, "All is safely gathered in"? But the well-loved Irish priest helped to get things into perspective.

"Farmers on Mendip have had a difficult time this year," he said, "but look around and see the fruit and vegetables and in the fields the grass is plentiful and green instead of dry and brown. God never fails. He has said, 'Seed time and harvest shall not fail'. If this is the worst harvest for sixty years, remember the fifty-nine good years in between. I wonder," he went on thoughtfully, for he never used notes, "did the farmers who blame God for this disastrous harvest remember to give Him thanks in good years — or did they take the credit to themselves?"

His words helped, and with the resilience of men who till the soil, Tom climbed out of despondency and began to plan the following year's work.

Shortly after the war, when the prisoners had been repatriated, labour problems decided Tom to invest in a milking machine. The day it was installed was sheer chaos. When the workmen had departed the cows were brought in and such bawling and mooing, such struggling and kicking ensued, that the womenfolk came from the house to see what was the matter. The animals resented the indignity of this new-fangled bit of machinery attached to their teats and many refused to let down their milk.

Tom scarcely slept a wink that night. "I'd *give* the wretched thing away," he muttered. In fact the cows soon settled to the new routine but Tom never really liked the machine, having been used, he said, to hand milking since he was "knee high to a grasshopper".

After VE Day and then VJ Day — victory in Europe followed by victory in Japan — the war was over, but life was regulated and rationed for a number of years. We stayed at the farm until 1967 when Tom retired. Now he returned to full-time nursing. We moved to our cottage on the slopes of Mendip and he took up full-time work at St John's Hospital, Axbridge. The hours were long, the work hard, but "I was never so happy in my life," said Tom.

CHAPTER NINE

Leaving the Farm

MY MOTHER CAME to visit us frequently during the last twelve years of her life. If it were in school time, Tom proved his genius with elderly folk as she became increasingly frail. At the weekends, particularly Saturdays, mother and I enjoyed ourselves together. She loved the sea, so in the morning we set off with flasks and sandwiches, a car full of rugs, wraps and books, for Weston-super-Mare. On the way we always stopped at a little village shop for our "secret" treat — an ice cream cornet, forbidden by her diabetic diet and therefore all the more enjoyable, and a Crunchie for me. Such small pleasures made Saturdays memorable.

At Weston I drove along the sands to the Uphill end of the beach and parked as near the water as possible, though the sea

With a Class at Cheddar Primary School

was usually so far out as to be scarcely visible beyond a large expanse of mud. Just occasionally it was high enough for me to have a shallow bathe.

Unless it was actually raining, my mother loved to sit in a garden chair muffled to the chin in rugs, with a book in her hands. Sometimes I sat and read, sometimes walked along the sands to the mouth of the river Axe. Here, if the tide was right, numerous yachts were being prepared by men and women, young and old, in yellow life-jackets, to set sail as soon as the water was high enough, and I watched their progress beyond Black Rock, past Brean Down and out to sea.

On mother's last visit we followed our Saturday routine. October came but, as it was sunny, we decided on one last picnic by the sea, although by now, my mother could scarcely walk. Access to the beach was by then free and a few cars were scattered along the beach. Having settled mother in her chair, I read for a while and then set off for a brisk walk along the sands.

Suddenly I realised that the sun had clouded over. With a sense of foreboding, I turned and hurried back. There was only one car on the beach! Engrossed in plans for a new short story, I had wandered too far. I raced towards the solitary figure seated beside the car, the sand soft beneath my feet. The wheels were sinking into the sand. With fast beating heart I helped my mother into the car, trying not to alarm her and looking round desperately for help.

Midway along the beach was a small caravan site on a promontory overlooking the sea. I ran as never before, praying that someone would be there at this, the end of the season. There was one man packing his caravan for winter storage, to whom I panted out my distress. There was a 'phone in the office, he said, but whether a garage would send a man out on a Saturday afternoon. . .? He went to the 'phone. Yes, a breakdown truck was on its way.

By now the wheels were half sunk, the line of the advancing tide rolled inexorably towards us under a lowering sky. Minutes ticked away as the wheels sank lower.

At last a yellow vehicle appeared. Two men applied chains and some lifting gear. With gurgling noises the car was released from the sucking sands and slowly, how slowly, the convoy crept forward. We reached the concrete ramp. I glanced back along our tracks. Already the tide was washing them away. "You were lucky," said one of the men. "There are cars sunk without trace beneath that sand."

Leaving the farm was not easy. During twenty-six years, through good times and bad, I had come to regard Mendip as my favourite spot on earth. On the way to school I would stop my Morris Minor, open the windows and listen. As the noise of the engine ceased the silence "surged softly in". Looking across "Little Switzerland" as local people called the stretch of hill and valley towards the strip of sparkling sea between Weston and Portishead, small sounds would emerge according to the season; the song of the lark, a distant curlew, the bleat of lambs responding to the baa-baa of their mothers, a cock crow from the farm across the valley. In summer the field bordering the road whispered as the light breeze gently stirred the ripening ears of corn.

Then came the steep descent of Hundred Acres Batch to Longbottom to join the Cheddar road. At this junction there was in autumn a breath-taking display of red and gold, yellow and bronze in the small wood beneath the pointed hill across the road, inviting one again to stop and stare. Just around the corner was a silver birch tree. Silver birches had always been a joy, but in autumn this was a revelation of gold coins on a silver tree.

Farther down this narrow gorge-road, bordered by limestone cliffs on the left and a steep wooded slope on the right, pale purple autumn crocuses grew on the bank and, lower down when the arching trees had been left behind, the fields were gemmed in summer with red, purple, and white anemones.

On Saturday afternoons my favourite walk was up Colliers Lane, over by Longhouse Barn, across Gruffy Ground to a stream which I called my river. Dressed in an old coat, woolly hat pulled over the ears, walking stick in hand, Tom said I looked like a tramp. But why worry? No one would see me. Boots allowed one to wade and the long coat was invaluable for protecting knees when crawling under barbed wire.

Wanstead Cottage, Shipham

In springtime, Gruffy Ground was ablaze with bluebells among delicate fronds of bracken, long-stemmed deep blue flowers, so different from the pallid little bells we had gathered so long ago in Wanstead Park. A walking stick was needed in Gruffy Ground, which was a series of humps and hollows remaining from the lead-mining days. Some of these were cone shaped and up to thirty feet deep and had to be wired round lest cattle should stray into the field and fall in. Tom told me one of his father's horses had fallen into a deep cleft when an old mining shaft caved in. Pigs of lead from Roman mines, marked with with emperors' names, have been found in fields near the amphitheatre still visible in Townsend Field, near Charterhouse Church, and the remains of buddling pools where the lead ore was washed and the flues which caught the volatile smoke from the burning ore, are still to be seen. During those walks I found fragments of mediaeval pottery in a newly ploughed field and flints shaped by Stone Age dwellers on Mendip before the Beaker Folk built Gorsey Bigbury.

The stream at the far end of the farm originated in the old red sandstone summit of Mendip, and emerged at the junction with the non-porous beds of shale. Crossing the road, it entered Gruffy Ground and to follow its twisty length was a perfect illustration in miniature of the development of a little river. Due to the dynamics of running water, in places the high banks were continually being eroded as the current cut away the lower strata, causing the grassy surface to collapse and be carried downstream. A little pile of stones placed on a perilously perched block, gave some indication as to how long it took the current to undermine the bank.

Sometimes the river bed narrowed and became overgrown and it was necessary to wade till the lie of the land allowed the stream to widen. Suddenly, rocky banks appeared: shale had given way to limestone.

Now came the most impressive part of the journey downstream. Fallen rocks jammed the watercourse and potholes appeared where a pebble had been swirled round and round in a hollow, forming a circular basin.

The end of the little river came dramatically as it plunged down a swallet in a high walled hollow, only to re-appear much lower down in Cheddar. It was fascinating to see how the swallets had lowered through the years as the bed of the stream was eroded, the present swallet being at least ten feet lower than one visible in the rocky wall.

In times of heavy rain, fresh fossiferous rocks were swept downstream, some polished smooth by the running water, some fossilised shells standing in relief where their limestone bed had been eroded. I only have to look at the stone-built fireplace in our cottage, to re-live days of solitude on Mendip: sunny days, days of gloom and mist. There was always something fresh to see by following the little river.

When the time came it was hard to give up such freedom even for the cottage halfway up the slopes of Mendip, but within weeks, Tom had returned to his chosen work of nursing.

And now a new chapter opened in the engrossing life of a village community.